LOVE WHAT GOD LOVES

SEEING ISRAEL THROUGH THE FATHER'S EYES

8-LESSON BIBLE STUDY COURSE

Fellowship of Israel Related Ministries

ISRAEL U

Copyright © 2025 IsraelU, a project of FIRM

Published by FIRM – Fellowship of Israel Related Ministries

All Rights Reserved. No part of this book may be reproduced or transmitted in any form or by any means, electronic or mechanical, including photocopying and recording, or by any information storage or retrieval system, except as may be expressly permitted in writing by the publisher, and except in the case of brief quotations embodied in critical reviews and certain other noncommercial uses permitted by copyright law. Requests for permission should be addressed in writing through FIRM Israel at www.firmisrael.org.

Unless otherwise noted, all Scripture quotations are taken from the (NASB®) New American Standard Bible®, Copyright © 1960, 1971, 1977, 1995, 2020 by The Lockman Foundation. Used by permission. All rights reserved. lockman.org.

Scripture quotations marked (NIV) are taken from the Holy Bible, New International Version®, NIV®. Copyright © 1973, 1978, 1984, 2011 by Biblica, Inc.™ Used by permission of Zondervan. All rights reserved worldwide. www.zondervan.com. The "NIV" and "New International Version" are trademarks registered in the United States Patent and Trademark Office by Biblica, Inc.™

Scripture quotations marked (ESV) are from The ESV® Bible (The Holy Bible, English Standard Version®), © 2001 by Crossway, a publishing ministry of Good News Publishers. Used by permission. All rights reserved.

Scripture quotations marked (KJV) are from The Authorized (King James) Version. Rights in the Authorized Version in the United Kingdom are vested in the Crown. Reproduced by permission of the Crown's patentee, Cambridge University Press.

Photographs & images are protected by copyright law. Resale or use of any images of this book is prohibited. Images © FIRM or © Adobe Stock, as noted.

IsraelU is a project of Fellowship of Israel Related Ministries, a US 501(c)3 tax-exempt organization based in Jerusalem, Israel.

ISBN: 979-8-218-64695-0

Editing, cover, and interior design by East Gate Editing.

Printed in the United States of America.

WATCH THE *LOVE WHAT GOD LOVES* TEACHING VIDEOS ON YOUR FAVORITE DEVICE.

SCAN THE QR CODE TO WATCH THE LESSON VIDEOS

GROUP LEADERS: A COMPLIMENTARY DIGITAL LEADER'S GUIDE FOR THIS COURSE IS AVAILABLE AT WWW.ISRAELU.ORG.

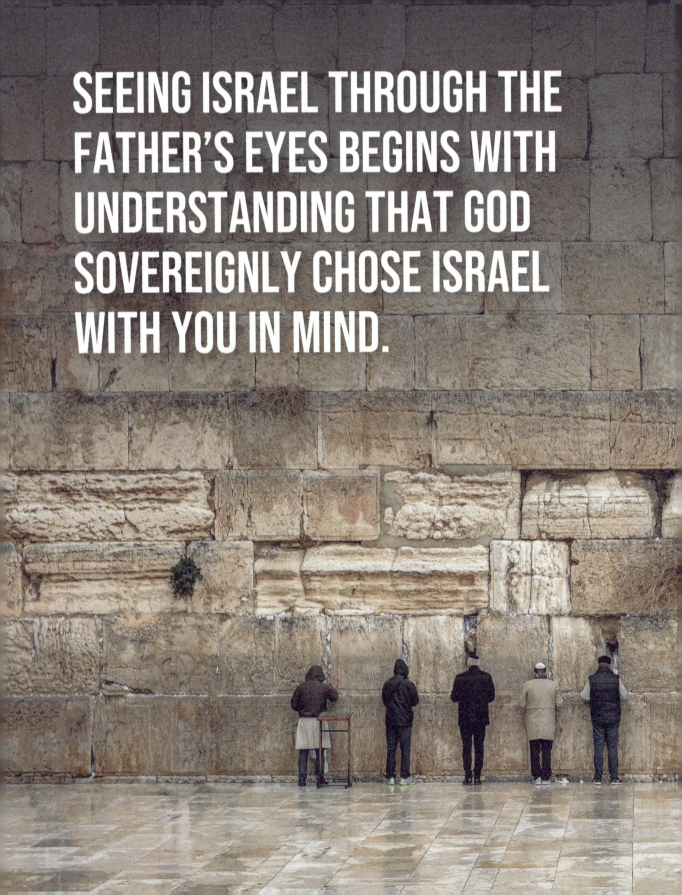

WELCOME TO THIS STUDY, *LOVE WHAT GOD LOVES: SEEING ISRAEL THROUGH THE FATHER'S EYES.*

We're so glad you've chosen to join us as we explore the Scriptures together and discover one of the primary keys to understanding the gospel narrative—Israel.

As believers, our hope is grounded in the *God of Israel* and the promises He has made to His people. And yet, we understand that Israel can be one of the most misunderstood topics for Christians today.

In this study, you will explore truths from a biblical worldview designed to help you navigate some of the questions surrounding Israel and the Jewish people.

The study presents the Israel story in concise, understandable, and unique ways that challenge prevailing narratives and connect us further to God's heart.

We want to provide a safe place to explore some biblical perspectives and align our hearts with the Father's. We believe that's where real transformation begins.

Over the next few weeks, you'll explore themes related to God's family—and how His choice of Israel reveals His heart for an international family. You'll study God's covenant-keeping nature and promises for restoration, even when the family gets messy and off-mission. You'll step into some difficult realities, like why so much controversy has surrounded the Jewish people throughout history and even the Church's rocky relationship with Israel.

Ultimately, you'll see the beautiful hope and future God has planned for Israel and for the nations and discover His invitation to embrace your role in this story.

When we see Israel through the Father's eyes and learn to love what He loves, God's salvation story—and our place within it—becomes clearer.

Until all Israel believes,

Michael & Vanessa

Michael & Vanessa Mistretta
Co-leaders of FIRM

TABLE OF CONTENTS

ABOUT THIS STUDY
   Course Description 9
   How to Use This Guide 10

LESSON 1: CHOSEN FOR PURPOSE: The Family of God 13
   Group Discussion Questions 15
   Personal Study Between Sessions
      DAY 1: Israel's Unique Call 17
      DAY 2: Abraham's Family Is God's Family 21
      DAY 3: Your Divine Purpose 28

LESSON 2: ESTABLISHED IN COVENANT: God Keeps His Promises . . . 33
   Group Discussion Questions 36
   Personal Study Between Sessions
      DAY 1: Believing for the Impossible 38
      DAY 2: God Is Faithful 41
      DAY 3: El Shaddai 45

LESSON 3: ONE STORY IN TWO TESTAMENTS: The Old Testament Still Matters 51
   Group Discussion Questions 54
   Personal Study Between Sessions
      DAY 1: The New Covenant 57
      DAY 2: The Great Exchange 61
      DAY 3: Israel Today 66

LESSON 4: WHAT HAPPENED TO THE ISRAEL GOD INTENDED? The Error of Replacement Theology 73
   Group Discussion Questions 76
   Personal Study Between Sessions
      DAY 1: Israel's True Identity 79
      DAY 2: How Are the Old Testament Promises to Be Applied? 84
      DAY 3: What Is Your Name? 88

LESSON 5: ISN'T HE OBVIOUS: Why It's Difficult for Jewish People to See Jesus 95
   Group Discussion Questions 98
   Personal Study Between Sessions
      DAY 1: The Sovereignty of God 100
      DAY 2: God's Mysteries 105
      DAY 3: God's Hidden Face Revealed in Joseph's Story 110

LESSON 6: JERUSALEM, JERUSALEM: The City of the Great King 115
   Group Discussion Questions 118
   Personal Study Between Sessions
      DAY 1: Mount Moriah – Chosen by God 121
      DAY 2: No Greater Love 127
      DAY 3: Jerusalem Will Be a Praise in the Earth 131

LESSON 7: ISRAEL'S FUTURE HOPE: The Coming Revival 137
   Group Discussion Questions 140
   Personal Study Between Sessions
      DAYS 1 & 2: The Coming Revival 143
      DAY 3: Hope in the Waiting 152

LESSON 8: WHAT'S OUR ROLE: The Not-So-Fine Print of the Great Commission 159
   Group Discussion Questions 162
   Personal Study Between Sessions
      DAY 1: To the Jew First 164
      DAY 2: Entering the Travail 169
      DAY 3: Shammah the Son of Agee a Hararite 173

ABOUT FIRM 178

ABOUT THE TRIBE 179

COURSE DESCRIPTION

Love What God Loves: Seeing Israel through the Father's Eyes is an 8-lesson course that takes you on a transformative journey into the heart of God by exploring Israel's vital role in His salvation story. Designed for small groups or individual study, this course reveals how a biblical understanding of Israel is key to unlocking the full narrative of Scripture and deepening your faith.

Throughout the course, you'll engage with 20-minute video teachings by Michael Mistretta that unravel God's eternal promises to Israel and their profound connection to your life. Each lesson is accompanied by powerful testimonies, a comprehensive study guide, and thought-provoking discussion questions that encourage meaningful dialogue and personal reflection.

We'll tackle common misconceptions about Israel, explore God's covenant-keeping nature, and discuss the controversies that have shaped the Church's relationship with the Jewish people. By the end of the course, you'll see how God's covenant with Israel directly connects to His faithfulness to you and His heart for the world.

Join us on this journey to see Israel through the Father's eyes, embrace your role in God's redemptive plan, and experience real transformation as you learn to love what He loves.

For further information about this course and other educational resources, visit israelu.org.

HOW TO USE THIS GUIDE

OVERVIEW

Love What God Loves is an 8-lesson course designed to be experienced in a small-group setting. It also works well for individual study, but we encourage you to invite some friends to join you and enjoy the process of learning together as you deepen community connection.

In your time together, utilize the *Getting Started* question(s) as a catalyst for group participation, watch the video, and then use any video notes and discussion questions to engage with the lesson topic. There may be more discussion questions than you have time for, but that's okay. Remember, the quality of your discussion is more important than the quantity of questions. The *Personal Study Between Sessions* section is provided for personal growth and a deeper look into the lesson content.

Group times are designed to run for about 90 minutes. You have the freedom to use the elements of the course as you see best. For those who appreciate a general guide for time, see the example 90-Minute Group Lesson.

90-MINUTE GROUP LESSON

- **10 min.** Welcome/refreshments
- **10 min.** *In Essence* summary and *Getting Started* question
- **20 min.** *Lesson Video*
- **40 min.** *Group Discussion Questions*
- **10 min.** *Conclusion & Prayer*

MATERIALS NEEDED

Everyone in your group will need a Bible and a copy of this study guide, which includes a place to take notes from the video teaching, discussion questions, and the *Personal Study* section. Everyone will have on-demand streaming video access, but for your group time, be sure to have access to the lesson video.

FACILITATION AND GROUP SIZE

Your group will need a person to take the group leader role and oversee the discussion, set up the video, and ensure the group's dynamics remain safe and time is honored.

A comfortable group size is between six and twelve people. If your group is larger, the group leader may choose to split it into two groups for the discussion questions to allow everyone ample time to share. Do what is best for your group.

PERSONAL STUDY BETWEEN SESSIONS

A *Personal Study* section is included to help participants engage with the subject matter during the week. This section includes Scripture reading and reflection questions to assist you in diving a bit deeper.

LESSON 1
CHOSEN FOR PURPOSE: THE FAMILY OF GOD

IN ESSENCE

As a loving Father, God desires an intimate relationship with us as His children. His plan to destroy the sin barrier and restore us to Himself is the central narrative of the Bible.

God orchestrated His salvation plan through Abraham and his family lineage, Israel. Israel is God's chosen vessel for service, entrusted with the good purpose of presenting the revelation of God and the hope of salvation through Jesus to the ends of the earth.

Seeing Israel through the Father's eyes opens our Bibles anew, revealing how precious we are to God.

GETTING STARTED

Group leader, read the In Essence *summary as you begin your time together. This will help set up the direction for this lesson.*

If your group members are just getting to know one another, take a few minutes to introduce yourselves and, as you do, answer this question:

On a scale of 1–10, how easy is it for you to be part of a group like this?

| ITS HARD! | 1 2 3 4 5 6 7 8 9 10 | I'M IN MY ELEMENT |

One more question before we move on:

▶ When you were younger, was there a treasure or an adventure you wanted so badly that you were willing to work, save, and sacrifice to get it? If so, what was it, and were you successful?

People are a treasure to God, and He desires to have a close relationship with us. Let's learn more about how God is establishing a family through the video teaching.

▶ LESSON 1 VIDEO

Group leader, stream the video lesson using the QR code on page 3.

As you watch the video teaching, use the following prompts and space provided to record anything that stands out to you.

1. When I began to see Israel through God's eyes, the Bible made a lot more sense.

   _____

   _____

2. Israel has been chosen not from preference or merit but for a divine purpose.

   _____

   _____

3. God chose to orchestrate His plan of salvation through one man, Abraham, and his family, Israel.

   _____

   _____

4. Israel's rebellion didn't derail God's choice of them or His salvation plan.

> *In you all the families of the earth will be blessed. (Gen. 12:3)*

   _____

   _____

5. God will be made known through imperfect vessels.

   _____

   _____

6. Israel was chosen to be . . .

   _____

GROUP DISCUSSION QUESTIONS

Group leader, read the following questions and prompts out loud and lead the discussion.

1. Michael told us that God's desire from the beginning has been to have a close relationship with His creation, and we see that demonstrated in the creation account (Gen. 1–3). Does God's desire and pursuit for a relationship resonate with you? Share a time with the group, if possible, when you knew God was drawing you closer.

    If this doesn't resonate with you, if you've not felt this reality, it's appropriate to say that as well.

2. How would you describe your current connection with Israel and the Jewish people? Below are some levels of connectedness to help you, but feel free to use your own description.

    > Not on my radar . . . primarily think of Israel in the biblical context . . . visited Israel because it's the land of the Bible . . . have Jewish friends/family, but we don't discuss religion . . . pray regularly for Jewish people to know Jesus as Messiah . . . I am Jewish

3. Most people are familiar with the term "chosen people" in reference to the Jewish people. Prior to this course, what did you understand the term to mean?

    What or who has most influenced your understanding on the topic?

4. Have someone read Deuteronomy 7:6–8 and Exodus 4:22. What do we learn about Israel in these verses? How are they described? What was the basis for God's choice?

5. For what central purpose did God choose Israel?

6. Michael said, "Israel isn't the source of our salvation; Israel is the vessel through whom God chose to work" (2 Cor. 4:6–7). Has God ever used an imperfect vessel to impart something good into your life? If so, what was that vessel? When have you been an imperfect vessel used by God for His purposes?

7. Israel's imperfection didn't invalidate God's choice. (We'll look deeper into this in later lessons.) What do you learn about God's faithfulness and tremendous love when considering Israel's calling and imperfection? How does this relate to us?

CONCLUSION

God wants a people—a family—for Himself, and He will have one. The relationship lost to sin in the garden of Eden is being restored through the death and life of God's Son, Jesus, the Messiah.

Jesus came through a people: Abraham's family. Israel was entrusted with the great responsibility of presenting God to all the families of the earth. They were chosen for service, and the light of God has shone forth through imperfect vessels. Jesus, the Perfect One, came through an imperfect family to reach other imperfect people with the hope of salvation and everlasting life. It's God's surpassing power on display, His renown.

Seeing Israel through the Father's eyes begins with understanding God sovereignly chose Israel with you in mind. Abraham's family is God's family.

CLOSE IN PRAYER

As you close your group's time together, see if anyone needs prayer, and take a few minutes to cover those requests.

You may also include thanking God for giving His Son, Jesus, for us. Thank God for raising up Israel, through whom Jesus has come. The Lamb of God is also the King of the Jews.

Pray for the Jewish people today, as their great call has come at a great cost. Pray for their salvation.

PERSONAL STUDY BETWEEN SESSIONS

This section is designed for your personal study to help you dig deeper into some of the themes from the teaching and discussion.

DAY 1

ISRAEL'S UNIQUE CALL

This week's lesson looked at Israel's chosenness. God called Israel a *segullah* (סְגֻלָּה) in Hebrew, meaning His "treasured possession." We saw that Israel was chosen for service not based on their merit or magnificence but simply because God is sovereign, and it was His loving will.

When the Bible writers referred to people in broad terms, there were only two categories: Israel and the nations—or said another way, Jews and Gentiles. Israel is not included in the Hebrew word *goyim* (גּוֹיִם), translated as "nations" or "Gentiles."

Before we're introduced in Genesis 12 to Abraham, the father of Israel, God specifically names the nations in Genesis 10, including Abraham's ancestors, the sons of Shem. Why is Israel separated or *chosen* from all other nations?

God will use Abraham's family, Israel, to bring the Messiah into the world and to reach all the families of the earth with the revelation of Himself. God chose Israel to serve and to be a witness and light to the nations. Their chosenness never guaranteed individual salvation, as each of us must receive forgiveness of

> **SEGULLAH** *means "treasured possession" and refers to the personal treasure a king acquired for himself and carefully preserved (Eccles. 2:8; Mal. 3:17).*

sin through faith in Jesus—that's true for all people regardless of what family a person is born into. But Israel was chosen as a servant nation.

God chose Israel with you in mind.

Jesus, the Messiah, took on human form and gave His life to provide for our salvation and destroy the works of the devil (Phil. 2:5–11; Heb. 2:14; 1 John 3:8). Jesus, whose name means "salvation," was born into a family—a people—divinely prepared for Him. Israel was that womb.

Look up the following and write out how each verse or passage describes Israel. Think about the roles or responsibilities God tasked Israel with.

1. Exodus 19:5–6
   Note: In ancient Israel, priests were intermediaries between God and the people of Israel—not to separate them but to bring the two together, ministers to both.

   _____

   _____

2. Isaiah 41:8–9

   _____

   _____

3. Isaiah 42:6

   _____

   Read Acts 13:47–49, where Paul connects this role to his ministry. What was the result of Paul and Barnabas being such a light?

   _____

4. Isaiah 43:10

   _____

Read Acts 1:8. What did Jesus call His followers?

JESUS – THE PERFECT REPRESENTATIVE

God called Israel to these roles, even though they were imperfect vessels, as we all are. Jesus, however, lived them perfectly.

> *Do not think that I came to abolish the Law or the Prophets; I did not come to abolish but to fulfill. (Matt. 5:17)*

5. Read these passages if time permits. They are a sampling of ways Jesus fulfilled the Law and the Prophets. There is so much more, though.

   Hebrews 7:21–28: Jesus, our faithful high priest
   Mark 10:43–45: Jesus, the servant of all
   John 8:12: Jesus, the Light of the world
   John 1:14, 18; 12:45; 14:9: Jesus, the witness of the Father

Jesus was the perfect representative of Israel. He fulfilled the Law, meaning He was sinless in keeping it, and He is the fulfillment of what was written. All the writers pointed to Him; every sacrifice and prophetic role had Him in mind!

To be clear, Jesus's fulfillment of the Law never negated Israel's chosen status as an instrument of God on earth. The Jewish people still have a purpose within the story of redemption, regardless of what it may look like today. We'll cover this more in upcoming lessons.

WITH YOU IN MIND

6. Read 1 Peter 1:10–12. How does Peter describe the Jewish prophets, and who does he say they were serving?

Read verses 18–20. For whose sake did Jesus, who is eternal, step into time at the prophesied time?

_____

Seeing Israel through the Father's eyes begins with understanding that God chose this nation as His servant, witness, and light—and to be the natural family of the Messiah—with us in mind so that we would come to know Jesus as our Savior and be reconciled to the Father.

REFLECTION

7. How have these truths influenced your understanding of Israel?

_____

_____

_____

8. Reflect on the enormity of God's love that He would move with such intentionality and extreme measure to reach you with the hope of salvation. Write out a prayer of thanksgiving to Him.

_____

_____

_____

FURTHER STUDY

To learn more about God's priority and purpose for Israel, scan this QR code to read Dr. Jack Hayford's article, "8 Biblical Reasons to Stand with Israel Today."

DAY 2
ABRAHAM'S FAMILY IS GOD'S FAMILY

Israel is Abraham's physical family through Isaac and Jacob, but that is not the full story for Abraham as a father.

In Paul's letter to the Romans, specifically chapters 4, 9, and 11, we learn more about Abraham's faith, what God promised him, and the broader picture of his family—and how that relates to you.

ROMANS 4: The Father of Faith

Read the following verses in Romans 4 and write out your answers to the questions.

1. In verses 1–3, how was Abraham justified, and what was credited to him, or (literally), "put to his account"?

   _____

   - The word "justified" in the Greek is *dikaloo* (δικαιόω). It is a legal term, a verb meaning "to remove the guilt, the liability to punishment." It declares the demands of justice have been satisfied.

   - The word "righteousness" comes from the same Greek root and means a person is in right standing with God. God's moral requirements are satisfied.

LESSON 1: CHOSEN FOR PURPOSE 21

Abraham's sin guilt was removed, and instead, God's righteousness was put to Abraham's account. Abraham was a believer, a man of faith! If you've come to God by faith in His Son, Jesus, this same legal transaction has taken place: your guilt has been removed, and His righteousness imputed. What a miracle!

2. In verse 13, what did God promise to Abraham and his descendants?

_____

Did you know that? We'll circle back to that promise at the end of Day 3. Let's continue and see how the promise will come and to whom.

3. Read verse 13 again and also verses 16–17.

   a. Will the promise of inheriting the earth come through works of the Law or through those of faith?

   _____

   b. Who are Abraham's descendants who will inherit the promise? Note the two groups of people listed in verse 16.

   In this context, those of the Law are of Jewish descent, and those of faith include Gentile believers.

   _____

   c. How is Abraham described?

   _____

Abraham has an international family! His physical family, Israel, and spiritual descendants—including those from Gentile nations.

Let's take a look at the Jewish side of the family before we return to consider the entire family.

ROMANS 9: The Israel within Israel

In Romans 9:1–5, Paul was writing about natural, physical Israel, whom he called "my kinsman according to the flesh." He added in verse 6, "For they are not all Israel who are descended from Israel." What does that mean?

Some scholars say it this way: "There is an Israel within Israel." Think in terms of natural and spiritual. *There is a spiritual family within Abraham's natural family.*

Not all of Abraham's physical descendants have shared his faith. Coming from Jewish descent sets a person into Abraham's physical family, but only saving faith in the Messiah qualifies anyone for Abraham's spiritual family.

For example, some Pharisees in Jesus's day boasted of having Abraham as their father but lacked any bit of saving faith. Jesus rebuked them and said they were of their father, Satan (see John 8:44). Those particular Pharisees were sons by birth but not sons by faith.

Paul calls Jewish believers within Abraham's physical family the "remnant" in Romans 11:5. They are the "Israel within Israel."

Within the Jewish side of Abraham's family, there are those who share in his faith (the Israel within Israel) and those who don't. *Some of Abraham's natural children are also spiritual children.*

Let's widen the scope again and consider Abraham's entire family—natural and spiritual. Paul illustrates it for us in Romans 11 by using the metaphor of an olive tree.

In the illustration, we'll see three groups.

- Jewish family members who share Abraham's faith
- Jewish family members who do not share his faith
- Gentiles who share Abraham's faith

ROMANS 11: The Olive Tree

Paul was speaking to the Gentile believers in the church at Rome (see v. 13).

Picture an olive tree with its natural branches and root system. In this metaphor, Israel is the olive tree.

4. Read Romans 11:17–18.

   a. What happened to *some* of the natural olive branches?

   _____

   b. What type of branch did Paul use to describe the Gentile believers ("you") in verse 17?

   _____

   c. What happened to the wild olive branch, and what benefit came to it?

   _____

   d. What warning did Paul give the wild branches in verse 18?

   _____

   e. Why were the wild branches not to be arrogant (or boastful) toward the natural branches?

   _____

What is the "rich root" or "nourishing sap" (Rom. 11:17) of this olive tree that is Israel? In botany we learn that every root anchors and nourishes the plant. What God-given gifts have anchored and nourished Israel? Let's see what Paul lists in the following verses.

5. Read Romans 9:3–5. God entrusted these things to the Jewish people for the spiritual benefit of all, the supreme gift being the Messiah (Christ): Jesus. He alone makes the root holy.

Back to Romans 11. In verse 18, Paul exhorted the Gentile believers that the root "supports you." The Greek word for "supports" is *bastazo* (βαστάζω), which means "to bear, to carry, to lift up." It carries the idea of a womb bringing forth life. Luke 11:27 uses the same word to refer to Mary's womb that carried and gave birth to Jesus.

This rich root has been a womb for the gospel of our salvation. Perhaps you've heard the phrase "the Jewish roots of our faith." This is where that idea comes from.

As wild olive branches, Gentile individuals who come to faith in Jesus are grafted into Abraham's family tree, and the life-giving sap from the root provides an anchor for our souls and spiritual nourishment.

Again, the supreme and central benefit, what everything points us to, is Jesus.

6. Read Romans 11:19–20, 23–25.

    a. Why are some natural branches broken off? (v. 20)

    b. Can they be grafted into the family tree spiritually?

    c. What is the "mystery" regarding Israel? (v. 25)

7. Read Romans 11:26–29.

    a. What will happen when the partial and temporary hardening over the Jewish heart is lifted? (vv. 26–27)

    b. Why will it be lifted? (vv. 28–29)

A day is coming when "all Israel will be saved" (v. 26), meaning the Jewish people living at that time will see and receive the Lord. At that time, Abraham's entire family will become a spiritual family—a family of faith. The natural and wild olive branches, representing the Jewish and Gentile brothers and sisters by faith, will be in place. God will have His family.

Abraham's family is God's family.

If you have believed and received Jesus as your Lord, if you've laid hold of the faith of Father Abraham, then this is your spiritual family (Rom. 4:22–25). Gentile believers don't become Jewish but are grafted into Abraham's family of faith. Abraham's family is an international family—a family from all nations.

REFLECTION

8. Which branch in the Romans 11 metaphor represents you? Circle the best description below.

    a. A natural branch (Jewish) who remains connected to the olive tree by faith
    b. A natural branch who has been cut off because of unbelief in Messiah, but who can be grafted in again
    c. A wild branch (Gentile) who has been grafted into the olive tree by faith
    d. A wild branch who has not yet been grafted into the family tree of faith

If your answer is either b or d, we invite you to come to the Father, through Jesus the Messiah, and be grafted into the family of faith. Consider these truths:

God so loved the world, that He gave His only begotten Son, that whoever believes in Him shall not perish, but have eternal life. (John 3:16)

The wages of sin is death, but the free gift of God is eternal life in Christ Jesus our Lord. (Rom. 6:23)

If you confess with your mouth Jesus as Lord, and believe in your heart that God raised Him from the dead, you will be saved; for with the heart a person believes, resulting in righteousness, and with the mouth he confesses, resulting in salvation. (Rom. 10:9–10)

A simple prayer of faith—agreeing that you are a sinner in need of a Savior and receiving the forgiveness of sins available only through Jesus's death and resurrection—will initiate your being grafted into this family tree of faith. If you have just prayed a prayer of faith, we rejoice with you and welcome you into the family of God, and we encourage you to share your decision with someone in your group.

9. Take some time to reflect on the truths you've seen in this lesson and write a prayer of response to God for what He has done on your behalf.

_____

_____

_____

_____

FURTHER STUDY

To learn more about the role of the Gentile within the olive tree, scan this QR code to read Eitan Shishkoff's article, "What Is a Gentile and Their Role in the Bible?"

> *Abraham's family is an international family—a family from all nations. Abraham's family is God's family.*

DAY 3
YOUR DIVINE PURPOSE

Today, we encourage you in your divine purpose. The mission given to the Jewish people hasn't changed—but the family has surely grown!

OUR SHARED MISSION

Read the passages below and write out your answers to the questions.

1. Matthew 28:19–20 and Acts 1:8. What instructions did Jesus give His disciples?

___

___

This mission to reach the world with the hope of salvation through Jesus is still the goal. This is God's family mission.

2. First Peter 2:5, 9–10. How does Peter describe the family of faith in these verses? *Note*: Peter is writing to both Jewish and Gentile believers living in the Roman Empire.

___

___

The mantle of calling entrusted to Israel has been extended over the shoulders of believing Gentiles as well. The wild olive branches grafted into the family tree share in the family mission of reaching the world with the gospel—not in place of Israel but alongside Israel, as co-heirs of the mission.

3. Ephesians 2:10 and 2 Corinthians 5:17–20. What has God prepared for us? What is the role of every believer?

4. Philippians 3:12–15. What do you think of Paul's passion to accomplish the mission God set before him? What was he willing to do with his past, and how would he approach the future?

How would you describe your passion and pursuit for what God has given you to do on His behalf?

5. What natural and spiritual gifts has God given you that you can use to reach others with the message of Jesus?

6. Are there hindrances that deter or distract you from living wholeheartedly for the mission? If so, write them out and pray about what to do about this.

_____

_____

_____

Everyone has individual and unique gifts and abilities to accomplish their calling. We are perfectly fashioned for the task, and we each must step out in faith with what He has put in our hands to fulfill what He has given us to accomplish.

THE PROMISE TO ABRAHAM'S HEIRS

In Day 2, we looked at the promise given to Abraham and his descendants recorded in Romans 4:13—the promise that Abraham's heirs will inherit the world. When Jesus returns at His second coming, He will establish the kingdom of God on earth and reign as King from Jerusalem. The prophets write about this. Jesus is King, but consider to whom He gives dominion, according to Daniel:

> *Then the sovereignty, the dominion and the greatness of all the kingdoms under the whole heaven will be given to the people of the saints of the Highest One; His kingdom will be an everlasting kingdom, and all the dominions will serve and obey Him. (Dan. 7:27)*

The saints of the Highest One are God's family, Abraham's family of faith. The promise of inheriting the earth and serving the Lord wholly will be upheld and fulfilled one day—maybe soon. Are we ready? Will you be ready?

7. Read Matthew 24:44–46. What will distinguish the servant as faithful and sensible when the master returns?

_____

REFLECTION

8. Read the *In Essence* lesson summary provided at the beginning of Lesson 1. As you have considered this topic of Israel's chosenness, have further questions come to mind? Or perhaps you've experienced poignant moments where some dots were connected. If so, write them out.

_____

_____

_____

_____

FURTHER STUDY

To learn more about the connection between Christians and Israel, scan this QR code to read Dr. Wayne Hilsden's article, "God's Plan: What Does the Bible Say About Israel?"

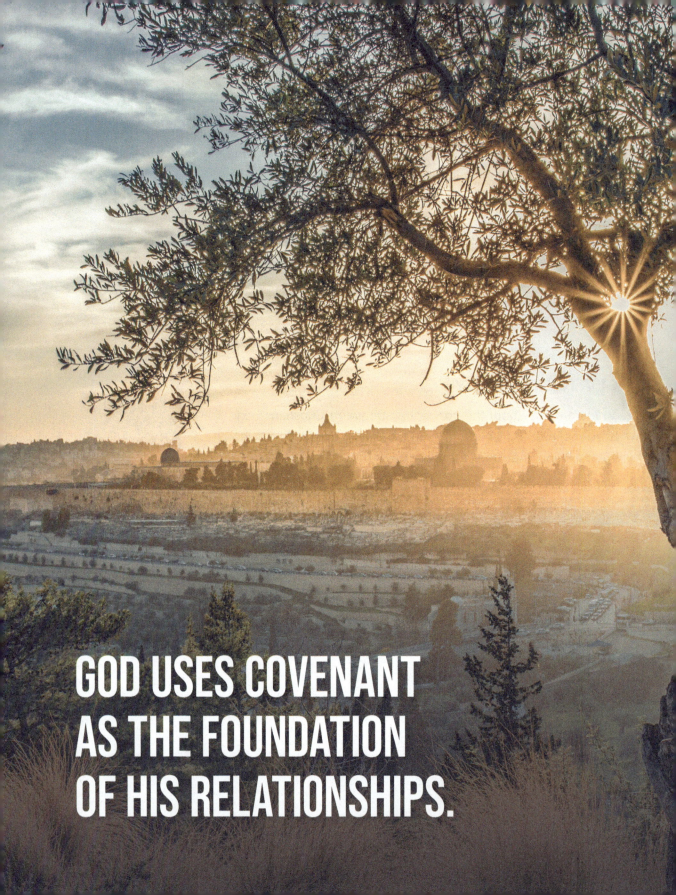

LESSON 2
ESTABLISHED IN COVENANT: GOD KEEPS HIS PROMISES

IN ESSENCE

God established His relationship with Israel through the Abrahamic covenant, an eternal agreement that God alone will uphold. God's unilateral and unconditional promise to Abram ensured his descendants would become a great nation, be blessed, be a blessing to all families on earth, and have a homeland. These covenant terms remain valid so long as the Lord is faithful.

The Abrahamic covenant laid the relational foundation through which God would establish a family—a people—for Himself. It formed Abraham's physical family, the Jewish people, and opened the door of hope to people from every nation who could be grafted into Abraham's family through faith.

The enduring chosenness of Israel as a servant nation is a proclamation to us, too, that we have a Father in heaven who keeps His covenants.

GETTING STARTED

Group leader, read the In Essence *summary as you begin your time together. This will help set up the direction for this lesson.*

As you open the group time, give everyone an opportunity to answer this question:

> ▶ What is one unique role you had in the family you were brought up in? (For example: oldest, baby, funny person, organizer, peacemaker, black sheep)

In the previous lesson, we looked at God's choice of Israel as a vessel for His purposes. Let's join Kayla and Michael again for the Lesson 2 Video segment, where we'll consider the question: *Is Israel still chosen?*

▶ LESSON 2 VIDEO

Group leader, stream the video lesson using the QR code on page 3.

As you watch the video teaching, use the following prompts and space provided to record anything that stands out to you.

1. In biblical times, when people entered into agreements, they did so by using a binding pledge called "covenant."

   _____

2. God uses covenant as the foundation of His relationships. Let's see the development of the Abrahamic covenant.

   a. Genesis 12

   Through a series of "I will" statements, God promised . . .

   _____

   b. Genesis 15

   The delay caused Abram to question.

   Abram believed God, and it was counted to him as righteousness.

   Cutting covenant . . .

   _____

   c. Genesis 17

   Abram would be the father of a multitude of nations.

   The Abrahamic covenant laid the foundation through which God would establish a family—a people—for Himself.

   _____

3. Is Israel still chosen?

   _____

4. The olive tree illustrates the family of God.

   I say then, God has not rejected His people, has He? May it never be! . . . This is My covenant with them . . . from the standpoint of God's choice they are beloved for the sake of the fathers; for the gifts and the calling of God are irrevocable. (Rom. 11:1, 27–29)

GROUP DISCUSSION QUESTIONS

Group leader, read the following questions and prompts out loud and lead the discussion.

1. Have you had to wait an extended time for something very important to you? If possible, share with the group about it.

   Is it hard or easy for you to wait?

2. Two times we see Abraham suggest to the Lord that the promised son might come through a means other than himself or Sarah. Who did Abraham suggest the promise might come through?

   a. Genesis 15:2–6

   b. Genesis 17:16–21

   How did the Lord respond to Abraham? What can we learn about the Lord here that we can apply to our relationship with Him?

> *Abraham awaited a promised son, Isaac, but he also saw the ultimate promised Son, the Messiah, Jesus, who would come through Abraham's family line.*

3. Let's look at the cutting of the covenant scene. Read Genesis 15:7–12, 17–18. We know it's the Lord who cut the covenant (v. 18) but notice how verse 17 describes the One who walked between the pieces.

   a. Read Ezekiel 1:1, 26–27, which describes "a man" on heaven's throne.

   b. Read Revelation 1:14–15, which describes Jesus as He appeared to John.

   What similarities do you see between these descriptions and the One who passed between the covenant pieces in Genesis 15:17? Who may it have been who walked the covenant path?

4. Read John 8:56–58. What did Jesus claim while speaking to the Pharisees?

5. Read Romans 4:17–24. What do we learn about Abraham's faith? What do we learn about God? What do we learn about anyone who believes in the Lord?

6. Read Psalm 105:8–11. According to these verses, and considering who walked through the covenant pieces, is the Abrahamic covenant still in effect? Is Israel still a chosen instrument?

> *The Abrahamic covenant was made with Abraham's physical family, Israel, and is open to anyone who will join through faith in Jesus.*

CONCLUSION

> *I will establish My covenant between Me and you and your descendants after you throughout their generations for an everlasting covenant, to be God to you and to your descendants after you. (Gen. 17:7)*

Is Israel still chosen for a unique purpose? Yes. The Father's relationship with Israel was established by an unconditional, everlasting covenant. The Lord alone walked between the covenant pieces; therefore, the covenant is valid—as long as the Lord is faithful to the terms. Will He be? You can bet on it! God is not done with Israel, and He's not done with us.

CLOSE IN PRAYER

As you close your group's time together, see if anyone needs prayer, and take a few minutes to cover those requests.

You might also take time to thank God for His faithfulness to His promises. For those in your group experiencing an extended season of waiting, encourage them by joining together in faith for what God will do on their behalf.

PERSONAL STUDY BETWEEN SESSIONS

This section is designed for your personal study to help you dig deeper into some of the themes from the teaching and discussion.

DAY 1

BELIEVING FOR THE IMPOSSIBLE

God often uses delay and impossible odds as refining tools to purify us from unbelief and self-sufficiency. God is working some things out of our character and working unshakable faith into us.

The prophet Habakkuk wrote, "The righteous will live by his faith" (2:4). This is a primary theme in Scripture as Paul quoted Habakkuk in Romans and Galatians, as did the writer of Hebrews.

1. Are you believing for something that is "impossible" in your own strength or ability, something that would be categorized as an "only God" provision? Write it below.

   _____

   _____

> *The righteous will live by his faith. (Hab 2:4)*

2. Read Habakkuk 2:2–4. Do what the Lord instructed Habakkuk and write out what the Lord has spoken to you. Record the vision. What do you see with eyes of faith that you haven't seen yet in the physical?

_____

_____

_____

_____

> *The LORD will fulfill his purpose for me; your steadfast love, O LORD, endures forever. (Ps. 138:8 ESV)*

3. Read Hebrews 11:8–16. What inspires you about Abraham's faith that you want to implement in your own life?

_____

_____

Abraham awaited the natural fulfillment of descendants and land, but in verses 10, 13–16, we see he also understood the much greater promise of a spiritual inheritance prepared for him. He saw the kingdom of God.

4. In Genesis 22, God tested Abraham's willingness to offer Isaac, the promised son, on an altar on Mount Moriah. Read Hebrews 11:17–19. What was Abraham sure of? What had the twenty-five years of delay and challenge forged in him?

_____

_____

REFLECTION

Over his life, we see Abraham's hope, doubt, and personal efforts to bring about the promise, his faith reestablished, and finally, unshakable faith. Does this process resonate with what you've experienced?

5. Read Acts 2:25–26. What is key to having unshakable faith? Where is your focus as you wait for your breakthrough?

_____

_____

_____

_____

6. What is the promise given in 1 John 5:4–5? Spend some time in prayer and ask the Lord to enlarge your faith, especially for your areas of concern.

_____

_____

▶ FURTHER STUDY

To learn more about God's covenant with Abraham in the Bible, scan this QR code to read the article by FIRM staff, "The Abrahamic Covenant: God's Promise to Abraham."

DAY 2
GOD IS FAITHFUL

When Abraham and Sarah fixed their eyes on themselves and their inabilities, they invented alternate plans to help God fulfill His promise (Gen. 15:2–3; 16:2; 17:17–18). When Peter shifted his eyes off Jesus and onto the crashing waves, he became unable to walk in the supernatural (Matt. 14:28–31).

We're no different. We're prone to the same self-sufficiency and fear that we read of in our favorite Bible characters.

In his last letter to Timothy, the apostle Paul gave this "trustworthy statement":

> *If we are faithless, He remains faithful, for He cannot deny Himself. (2 Tim. 2:13)*

It's important for us to lock this truth into the core of our being: *God is faithful.*

1. Look up the following verses and write out what you learn about the Lord.

    a. Lamentations 3:21–23

    b. Psalm 36:5

c. Hebrews 10:23

_____

d. 1 Thessalonians 5:24

_____

e. 2 Thessalonians 3:3

_____

We've looked at Abraham's faith—now let's consider Sarah's and see how she tethered her faith to God's ability to keep His word.

> *For nothing will be impossible with God. (Luke 1:37)*

2. Read Genesis 18:1–15 and answer the questions that follow.

Who came to Abraham and Sarah's tent? (It says three men, but one of them is identified in verse 1.)

_____

Remember these previous appearances:
- The Lord appeared to Abram in Genesis 12:7.
- The Lord walked through the covenant pieces in Genesis 15:17.
- The Lord appeared to Abraham in Genesis 17:1.

Abraham knew what the Lord looked like! It's no wonder he ran to Him and bowed.

How did Sarah respond in verse 12 to the Lord's announcement? Why do you think she responded that way?

_____

_____

What rhetorical question did the Lord ask in verse 14?

3. Before we're tempted to criticize Sarah for her laughter, let's go to Hebrews 11:11 and see what is written of her there. Did she believe the Lord? According to the last phrase in verse 11, what was her faith based on?

REFLECTION

4. Impossible odds, fear, outside voices, horrible circumstances . . . these are some obstacles that can threaten our resolve to believe God will come through. What challenges have you had to overcome to maintain hope?

Are you facing a current obstacle? If so, what?

5. Read Romans 5:2–5. How can we rejoice in hope? Be sure to follow the progression in these verses.

_____

_____

_____

Why does hope not disappoint? (v. 5)

_____

_____

> *Those who hope in me will not be disappointed.*
> *(Isa. 49:23 NIV)*

It's encouraging to find Abraham and Sarah in the Hebrews 11 list of those with remarkable faith because we've seen their stories and know they weren't perfect. We relate to that!

The Lord isn't looking for perfect people but faithful ones. Let's lay hold of the "trustworthy statement"—*He remains faithful.*

▶ FURTHER STUDY

To learn more about hope and faith in the Bible, scan this QR code to read Casey Tait's article, "Hope in the Bible: Faith, Waiting & Remembrance for Israel."

DAY 3
EL SHADDAI

There are many names for God throughout the Old Testament, and each one sheds light on His attributes. The Lord reveals Himself through His name, and it is always the precise quality needed in each situation.

Twenty-five years after the Lord established a covenant with Abraham, the Lord appeared to him as "God Almighty" or in Hebrew, *El Shaddai* (אֵל שַׁדַּי). The apostle John said no one has seen God the Father at any time, but *El Shaddai* is the divine entity that men and women are allowed to see. Who is He?

Let's consider the first recorded appearance of *El Shaddai* in Genesis 17:1–3.

1. How did Abram respond when *El Shaddai* introduced Himself?

   _____

   _____

The word *El* is an ancient term widely used to refer to deity. *Shaddai* speaks of God's might or power and can be understood as "all-sufficient." We might be tempted to think brawn or someone able to inflict violence, but this word doesn't speak to that. Instead, the Hebrew root word *shad* means "the breast."

El Shaddai can be understood as "the breasted one," carrying also the attribute of "almighty." Think of the nourishing, life-giving milk that comes from a mother's breast and the nurturing care she provides to a crying baby. Think of the father who draws his child into his strong chest to comfort, protect, and assure.

God Almighty, or *El Shaddai*, is used seven times in the Old Testament and is known as the covenant name of God until the time of Moses.

Abraham and Sarah were still without a son twenty-five years after the promise was given. They had waited a long time and most likely, there were days filled with discouragement. If anyone needed *El Shaddai* to comfort and love, to bring forth life and provide through His great power, it was them. Abram fell on his face before *El Shaddai*, God Almighty— the all-sufficient one.

2. From his place of personal pain, Paul wrote about his "thorn in the flesh." Read 2 Corinthians 12:9–10. What did the Lord tell Paul, and what was his response?

   a. Write out the last phrase in verse 10.

   b. Is there an area of your life where you feel weak and need His strength? If so, what is it? Can you accept that His grace is sufficient for you?

3. Read also 2 Corinthians 9:8, Ephesians 3:20, and 2 Peter 1:2–3. What is God able to do for us?

REFLECTION

4. What does it mean to you that your God is *El Shaddai*, "the breasted one"? Have you longed to be brought near, truly loved, nourished, and protected? Do you need His almighty power today? How so?

   _____

   _____

   _____

   _____

5. Read Psalm 91:1–4, and write out what you learn about the Almighty, or *El Shaddai*.

   _____

   _____

   _____

   _____

   As Abraham did, bow before Him in prayer and allow Him to speak to you. Write out below what you sense the Lord saying.

   _____

   _____

   _____

   _____

6. Read the *In Essence* lesson summary provided at the beginning of Lesson 2. As you have considered this topic of God's covenant faithfulness, have further questions come to mind? Or perhaps you've experienced poignant moments where some dots were connected. If so, write them out.

___

___

___

___

The enduring chosenness of Israel, God's faithfulness to His covenant with Abraham, is a resounding proclamation that we have a Father in heaven who keeps His word. If God keeps His promises to Israel, we can be assured He will keep His word to us.

▶ FURTHER STUDY

To learn more about God's plan for Ishmael in the Bible, scan this QR code to read Kathi Shaw's article, "Is Ishmael Part of the Abrahamic Covenant?"

NOW THESE THINGS HAPPENED TO THEM AS AN EXAMPLE, AND THEY WERE WRITTEN FOR OUR INSTRUCTION. (1 COR. 10:11)

LESSON 3
ONE STORY IN TWO TESTAMENTS: THE OLD TESTAMENT STILL MATTERS

IN ESSENCE

The entire Bible is one story, revealing God's plan to redeem us from sin's penalty and power and restore us to a right relationship with Him. His salvation purposes declared in the Old Testament are fulfilled in the New.

Embracing the entire Word of God allows us to see His redemption story and capture the true picture of what God is doing presently with Israel and the nations. He has declared the end from the beginning (Isa. 46:10) that we might know Him and live victoriously.

If we neglect the Old Testament, we're left with an incomplete picture of God, His purposes, Israel, and our shared future.

GETTING STARTED

Group leader, read the In Essence *summary as you begin your time together. This will help set up the direction for this lesson.*

As you open the group time, give everyone an opportunity to answer this question:

▶ If someone were to make a documentary of your life, what would be your favorite scene?

We all have moments in our lives that are fun to retell and others we prefer to forget, but our stories are incomplete without every scene. The same is true with the story God is writing. Let's join the video lesson as we consider how the Bible, with its sixty-six books, tells one story.

▶ LESSON 3 VIDEO

Group leader, stream the video lesson using the QR code on page 3.

As you watch the video teaching, use the following prompts and space provided to record anything that stands out to you.

1. Jesus spoke of Himself as the main character in the Hebrew Scriptures.

2. Where do we see Jesus revealed in the Old Testament?

    - Theophanies
    - Types and foreshadows
    - Prophecies

3. God's eternal plan is revealed first in the Old Testament.

4. God's purposes declared in the Old Testament come about in the New Testament.

5. If we neglect the Old Testament, we can develop a skewed picture of Israel.

> *The same prophets who prophesied Israel's chastisement for sin prophesied their restoration.*

GROUP DISCUSSION QUESTIONS

Group leader, read the following questions and prompts out loud and lead the discussion.

1. Which of these is closest to describing your current level of interaction with the Old Testament?

    a. I never read it
    b. I read it sometimes but am unsure how it relates to me
    c. I read parts of it, like the Psalms and Proverbs
    d. I read it frequently and would like to understand it better
    e. I love it and read it regularly

2. Have you viewed the Bible as one continuous story or two independent testaments? What or who has influenced your view?

3. Read 1 Corinthians 10:11. Michael said the events and people in the Old Testament were literal and simultaneously used as illustrations or foreshadows of spiritual truths for our benefit. What do you think about that statement? Does it reflect your personal view?

   If there is, or was, a level of disinterest or some disconnect to the Old Testament for you, what cause(s) attributed to that?

4. Read Acts 10:43, Hebrews 10:7, and Luke 24:25–27, 44. The entire Bible is about Jesus. Briefly share some Old Testament revelations or prophecies of Jesus that come to mind.

   According to Luke 24:45, if you want to see Jesus and the gospel message more thoroughly in the Old Testament, what could you ask of the Lord?

5. Describe a time when God sovereignly opened your eyes to a spiritual truth. What impact has that had?

6. Read Isaiah 56:3, 6–8. Israel is the nation to whom Isaiah wrote, and the children of Israel are the primary people to whom the Lord spoke, so who are the "foreigners"?

    a. Read also the following two verses and answer the questions.

        - Isaiah 49:6: Is the message of Messiah for the tribes of Jacob (Israel) only?

        - John 10:16: Jesus was speaking to a Jewish audience, so who are the "other sheep"?

        - What message is the Lord giving?

    b. What does this tell you about God's eternal plan? What does knowing that God's eternal plan has always had you in mind mean to you?

7. Read the following sentences and discuss the idea within your group. Do you agree? Disagree? Are you unsure?

    The Israel of the Old Testament is the same Israel in the New Testament, and the Jewish people worldwide and the nation of Israel today are a continuation of biblical Israel. It's one story.

CONCLUSION

The Bible was penned by about 40 authors over approximately 1,400 years using two primary languages—yet it tells one harmonious story because it is truly authored by God, who inspired men to write on His behalf. We want to be people who embrace and prioritize the entire Bible as one message from the Father to us.

We need the full revelation of Jesus and to understand God's complete plan, which enables us to stand strong both today and in the critical days ahead. In this course, as we seek to see Israel through the Father's eyes, let's understand His dealings with them from Genesis to Revelation.

CLOSE IN PRAYER

As you close your group's time together, see if anyone needs prayer, and take a few minutes to cover those requests.

You might also pray for an increase of hunger and understanding for the Scriptures. The entire Bible, Old and New Testaments, points to Jesus. Let's find Jesus and the gospel message in every part.

> *Open my eyes, that I may behold wonderful things from Your law.* (Ps. 119:18)

> *Then He opened their minds to understand the Scriptures.* (Luke 24:45)

There isn't an Old Testament plan and a different New Testament plan. There is one eternal plan of God to reach the world with the gospel.

PERSONAL STUDY BETWEEN SESSIONS

This section is designed for your personal study to help you dig deeper into some of the themes from the teaching and discussion.

DAY 1
THE NEW COVENANT

God uses covenant as the foundation of His relationships. We looked at the Abrahamic covenant in the previous lesson, which is foundational to God forming the people through whom the Messiah would come and their land inheritance.

The Abrahamic covenant also opened the door for other covenants between God and Israel:

- **The Mosaic covenant**, also known as the Mosaic law, instructed Israel on how to live as a nation in the promised land. It revealed God's holiness and exposed Israel's sin and need for a savior. It was a conditional covenant—meaning Israel could break it and lose occupancy of the land, which is what happened. The children of Israel maintain the inheritance of the land because it was established in the unconditional Abrahamic covenant, but they lost occupancy for many years (Lev. 26:40–44; Ezek. 37:21–28).

- **The Davidic covenant** identified the specific family within Israel through whom the Messiah would be born. God promised David his son would reign as king *forever* from Jerusalem. Jesus, the (generations later) Son of David, was born King of the Jews, died King of the Jews, and will return as the Lion of Judah and King of kings! (1 Chron. 17:11–15; Matt. 1:1).

- **The new covenant** is the covenant of our salvation, establishing a people from every nation who receive the forgiveness of sins, enter a relationship with God as sons and daughters by faith, and receive a new identity and eternal life.

Let's look at the new covenant more closely as we consider the theme this week of seeing the message in the Bible as one story. How do we see the new covenant in both testaments?

1. Read Jeremiah 31:31–34. With whom was the new covenant made (vv. 31, 33)?

Does that surprise you? Many assume the new covenant is a plan established with the Church in the New Testament, but at its foundation, God made this covenant with Israel.

2. Read the verses in the chart below and write out what you learn about the new covenant. This will be a cursory look at a much larger topic.

   Note: In the Jeremiah and Hebrews passages below, the new covenant is contrasted with the Mosaic covenant, or the Mosaic law.

	NEW COVENANT
Jeremiah 31:33–34 Isaiah 59:20–21	Provisions:
Ezekiel 36:25–27	Provisions:

58   LOVE WHAT GOD LOVES

Hebrews 7:22; 8:6	Who is the mediator, and how is the covenant described?
Hebrews 9:11–12 1 Peter 1:18–20	Covenants required the shedding of blood. Whose blood was shed? What did it obtain? How is the blood described?
Ephesians 2:8–9 Romans 10:9	How does a person enter the new covenant and receive all these benefits?

Jesus said to him, "I am the way, and the truth, and the life; no one comes to the Father but through Me." (John 14:6)

3. According to Hebrews 9:26, why did Jesus appear?

4. Now read Hebrews 9:14. What is cleansed or purified by the blood of Jesus?

Jesus has appeared to put away our sin, but His work on the cross also cleanses our conscience. In other words, we are washed clean of our sin, but *we also know it.*

We need to know it. We can know it, friend. *Do you know it?* You've been washed clean!

Let your mind agree with this spiritual reality. The same sin condition that was rendered washed away in heaven's courtroom must likewise be recognized in the courtroom of your mind.

The power of God's forgiveness is why Paul could write:

Therefore, if anyone is in Christ, he is a new creation; the old has gone, the new has come! (2 Cor. 5:17 NIV)

Therefore there is now no condemnation for those who are in Christ Jesus. (Rom. 8:1)

REFLECTION

Use the space below to write out your thoughts regarding the new covenant blessings as yours if you belong to Jesus. If you struggle to embrace the truth that you've been washed clean, write that out, and be specific. Where is the hangup? Invite the Holy Spirit to speak to you. Take time to listen to His response.

_____

_____

_____

_____

_____

 ## FURTHER STUDY

To learn more about how the new covenant connects to Passover—and to you—scan this QR code to read Doug Hershey's article, "The Last Supper and First Communion at Passover."

DAY 2
THE GREAT EXCHANGE

A common feature of biblical covenants was the exchange of personal items. Let's look at a cameo of the covenant between Jonathan and David and connect some dots to corresponding New Testament truths.

Keep in mind our theme in this lesson of seeing the continuous story throughout the Bible. It's been said the truths concealed in the Old Testament are revealed in the New. Paul wrote what was in shadow form in the Old finds its substance in Jesus (Col. 2:17).

What do we learn about our covenant relationship with Jesus when we look at Jonathan and David's commitment to one another?

1. Read 1 Samuel 18:1–4. We don't have all the details of the cutting of covenant, but we have exactly what the Holy Spirit wants us to have. What personal items did Jonathan give David as their covenant was formed?

   _____

   _____

   When two people made a covenant of friendship, the relationship superseded all other human relationships. The covenant partners were done with independent living and committed themselves to one another. It was more than saying, "We were friends one summer, so let's continue the friendship," but "You are not alone! Your burden is mine. Your fight is mine. Your joy is mine. Your family is family to me. Your protection and well-being are my concern. I live and make decisions with you in mind."

2. Read 2 Corinthians 5:15. As people who are in relationship with Jesus through the new covenant, how are we to live?

   a. Are you done with independent living? Do you live with Him in mind? Make decisions with Jesus in mind? Is His burden yours? His family? How does this truth settle with you?

   _____

   b. Is there an area of your life where you've maintained independent control, an area you need to surrender? If so, which one(s)? Will you do it today?

   _____

   _____

Let's look at the personal items Jonathan gave to David in 1 Samuel 18:4 and the corresponding truths those items speak of in our covenant relationship with Jesus. Again, what is in shadow form in the Old Testament finds its substance in Jesus. It's one story, pointing us to Him and His work of salvation on our behalf.

3. The robe

   a. Old Testament shadow:

   The robe spoke of identity. To put on the robe of a covenant partner expressed oneness with that person—"What's his is mine. We are one."

   Isaiah, likening the garments to wedding clothes and underscoring the idea of oneness, wrote that the Lord has clothed (us) with garments of salvation, with a robe of righteousness (Isa. 61:10).

b. New Testament substance:

He [God] made Him [Jesus] who knew no sin to be sin on our behalf, so that we might become the righteousness of God in Him. (2 Cor. 5:21)

Jesus took upon Himself our robe of sin, our guilt and shame, and in exchange, robed us with His righteousness. What an exchange!

In Luke 15:22, when the repentant prodigal son returned home, his father called for the best robe to be placed upon him. The son's identity, the relationship, was restored.

Romans 13:12–14: What are we to lay aside, and what are we to put on?

_____

Luke 24:49: What are we to be clothed in?

_____

Colossians 3:9–14: What attributes are part of our "new self"?

_____

4. The armor (including his sword and bow)

a. Old Testament shadow:

The exchange of armor was a way to express, "Your enemies are mine. You are not alone in battle, but I will arise in your defense and seek your victory. I have your back."

b. New Testament substance:

We have the full power of the Godhead on our side when we are in covenant with Jesus. Imagine it! As Paul says in Romans 8:31, if God is for us, who can be against us?

Ephesians 6:10–13, 16–17: What "spiritual armor" has God given us, and what is Paul's repeated exhortation to the one in battle?

_____

_____

First Peter 5:8–10: What will the Lord do for us as we stand against Satan?

_____

5. The belt

   a. Old Testament shadow:

   In David's day, the belt held the sword and arrows. It speaks of strength and resource. Jonathan was saying to David, "When you need me, I will be there with all my strength and ability. My resources are at your disposal." The belt holds the essentials and keeps them at hand.

   b. New Testament substance:

   It's never comfortable to feel weak, even at the end of ourselves, but the Lord met Paul there and assured him (and us) that His power is perfected in our weaknesses (2 Cor. 12:9–10). Do you lack strength, ability, or resources today? Jesus stands with you with His full supply.

   Isaiah 11:5: These verses speak of the Messiah, Jesus. How is His belt described?

   _____

   Ephesians 6:14: How is the belt of God's armor described?

   _____

Philippians 4:13: What is the outcome when we are united with Jesus's strength?

REFLECTION

If you are in the new covenant with Jesus, you have received His robe, His armor, and His belt. His grace is truly sufficient for you.

6. What do you need most from Jesus, your Covenant Partner, today? The robe? The armor? The belt? How so? It's all there for you.

And my God will supply all your needs according to His riches in glory in Christ Jesus. (Phil. 4:19)

Great job today. There was a lot to read and consider, but the truths can be life-transforming as we fully embrace the extraordinary sacrifice and provision of Jesus through the new covenant. We encourage you to take what you've learned and share it with others.

FURTHER STUDY

To learn more about this topic, scan this QR code to read the article by FIRM staff, "Battle Strategies: Finding Victory in Uncommon Places."

DAY 3
ISRAEL TODAY

So far in Lesson 3, we've seen that God has authored one harmonious story from Genesis to Revelation. We want to embrace the entire Bible. If we neglect either testament, we end up with a skewed understanding of His story.

Jesus is the supreme figure in both testaments. God's plan of salvation is the same in both testaments.

Today, we will answer two questions: *Is Israel the same in both testaments? And are the Jewish people today a continuation of biblical Israel?*

ISRAEL IN THE OLD TESTAMENT

1. Read Genesis 35:9–12. Who is Israel and how did he get his name? What did God promise him?

   _____

   _____

   Jacob's twelve sons became the twelve tribes of Israel. Israel was a man, then a nation, as the family grew.

ISRAEL IN THE NEW TESTAMENT

There were about 400 years between the close of the Old Testament and when Jesus was born. The question is: *Is the Israel of the New Testament a continuation of Israel in the Old Testament?* It may seem obvious to answer yes, but let's confirm it.

2. According to Matthew 1:1–2, who were Jesus's ancestral fathers? Was Jesus born into the same Israel as the Israel of the Old Testament?

   _____

   _____

Below are a few examples that confirm Jesus, the disciples, and the apostle Paul saw themselves as part of the same national Israel and divine purpose founded in the Old Testament:

- Jesus's death on the cross was the blood that ratified the new covenant God made with Israel.
- Jesus said the entire Old Testament speaks of Him and that He came to fulfill the Law and the Prophets (Matt. 5:17).
- At Pentecost, Peter addressed the crowd as "men of Israel," "brethren," and "house of Israel" (Acts 2).
- After the birth of the Church, Stephen recited Israel's history in Acts 7, beginning with: "Hear me, brethren and fathers! The God of glory appeared to our father Abraham" (v. 2).

3. Read Philippians 3:5. How did Paul, the greatest apostle and church planter, describe himself?

   _____

The Israel of the New Testament is the same Israel of the Old—the same familial identity, living on the same land, with the same mission.

ISRAEL TODAY

What about today? Are today's Jewish people worldwide and the nation of Israel a continuation of biblical Israel?

_____

_____

Why ask the question—does it matter? *It does.*

- There is an Israel prophesied throughout Scripture whose people will return to their original homeland and then return to the Lord. There is a physical and spiritual restoration for Israel.
- Jesus said in Matthew 23:37–39 that His second coming would be to a Jerusalem, an Israel, whose leadership will welcome Him and declare, "Blessed is He who comes in the name of the Lord!" (v. 39).
- Paul wrote there will be a day when "all Israel will be saved" (Rom. 11:26), a national turning to the Lord. *Who is that Israel?*

In AD 70, Jerusalem was destroyed by the Romans, and by AD 135, the Jewish people were banished from Judea. They scattered into the four corners of the earth, just as the Jewish prophets prophesied. Although there has always been some Jewish presence in the Land, even if small, the Jews remained primarily in exile until 1948. Then, by the hand of God, Israel became a sovereign nation once again, and the doors were open for Jewish people from around the world to make their way home—and their return continues today.

In Genesis 10:5, 20, and 31, we learn the components of a nation: family, land, and language.

- Regardless of the attempts to annihilate the Jewish people over the millennia, the Jewish people live. The Jewish family is growing.
- Besides Israel, no other people in history have had a homeland, been exiled for 2,000 years, and returned to that same land.

- Besides Israel, no other people in history have had a language, lost the language in exile, and had the same language resurrected as a mother tongue simultaneous to their return to their homeland.

It's a miracle! The Jewish people living outside of the nation of Israel today are still the sons and daughters of Abraham, Isaac, and Jacob, even while being productive citizens of other nations.

Is it *this Israel* of whom the ancient prophets spoke who will return to the Lord and welcome the Messiah, Jesus, in the latter days?

No one knows the day or hour of the prophetic fulfillments, of course, but is modern Israel, including the Jewish people worldwide, those who will see and take part in the fulfillment of the ancient prophecies concerning Israel? We believe so. *Who else could it be?*

4. Read Hosea 3:4–5 and write out what was prophesied about Israel and the general timing of the fulfillment noted in verse 5.

5. Read Jeremiah 30:3. What is promised?

6. Read Jeremiah 31:1–4, 7–11, 14. What is prophesied for Israel in these verses? *Note:* Jeremiah 30:24 identifies the timing as "in the latter days."

There is much to consider here! If you believe modern Israel is a continuation of biblical Israel, it ought to impact how you pray for and interact with the people. No nation is perfect, certainly, but let's be diligent to see Israel through the Father's eyes. The Scriptures are still speaking—all of them!

REFLECTION

7. Read the *In Essence* lesson summary provided at the beginning of Lesson 3. As you have considered how the Old Testament still matters, have further questions come to mind? Or perhaps you've experienced poignant moments where some dots were connected. If so, write them out.

_____

_____

_____

_____

_____

_____

_____

The Bible is one continuous story. If we neglect any part, we're left with an incomplete picture of God, His eternal purposes for all people, and of Israel and our shared future.

▶ FURTHER STUDY

To learn more about how Israel relates to you as a believer, scan the QR code below for a short video by FIRM, "Why Israel: How Your Christian Faith Is Rooted in Jesus and the Jewish People."

LESSON 4
WHAT HAPPENED TO THE ISRAEL GOD INTENDED? THE ERROR OF REPLACEMENT THEOLOGY

IN ESSENCE

Satan is in the identity theft business. He distorted Israel's God-given identity by introducing a false doctrine into the early Church called Replacement Theology. For centuries, this doctrine has been a destructive tool, causing division and great pain both within the Church and between the Church and the Jewish people.

Replacement Theology is the belief that due to Israel's sin, God has rejected Israel as His chosen people. The position asserts that Israel's unique role in redemptive purposes and the divine promises that bear their name have been transferred to the Church.

Replacement Theology undermines God's covenant faithfulness and desire for a unified family, resulting in indifference toward Jewish salvation and fostering antisemitism within the Church. Just as Israel has been partially blinded from seeing her Jewish Messiah, much of the Church has been blinded to God's enduring plan for Israel.

The family of God is reawakening to see Israel through the Father's eyes—not as rejected or replaced but loved and with a future.

GETTING STARTED

Group leader, read the In Essence *summary as you begin your time together. This will help set up the direction for this lesson.*

As you open the group time, give everyone an opportunity to answer this question:

> ▶ Whose identity would you like to borrow for a day, and what would you do in those twenty-four hours?

It's important to stay true to who God has made us. Let's join the lesson and learn more about a strategic threat to Israel's identity that has had significant impact over hundreds of years.

▶ LESSON 4 VIDEO

Group leader, stream the video lesson using the QR code on page 3.

As you watch the video teaching, use the following prompts and space provided to record anything that stands out to you.

1. Satan is in the identity theft business.

   _____

   _____

2. Satan introduced a dangerous doctrine into the Church called Replacement Theology, which presents an altered view of both Israel and the Church.

   _____

   _____

3. "I will pursue, I will overtake, I will divide the spoil."

   _____

   _____

4. By distorting Israel's identity, Satan could divide the Church.

   _____

   _____

> Gentile Church leaders concluded that God had rejected national Israel. If God rejected Israel, then the Church would do the same.

5. With the identity theft, new terms came into play within the Church.

   _____

   _____

LOVE WHAT GOD LOVES

6. The Church, composed of Jewish and Gentile believers, distanced herself from her Jewish roots and persecuted the Jewish members.

7. The allegorical method of Bible interpretation was taken to the extreme.

> *The Old Testament can't only be for Israel, and it can't only be about the Church. It's literally true and spiritually applicable.*

8. Replacement Theology has tragic implications.

9. "Pursue, overtake, and recover all."

10. All God has declared over Israel and the Church will come about. What the enemy has stolen will be recovered because of Jesus's victory.

> *Just as Israel has been partially blinded from seeing her Jewish Messiah, much of the Church has been blinded to God's enduring plan for Israel.*

LESSON 4: WHAT HAPPENED TO THE ISRAEL GOD INTENDED?

GROUP DISCUSSION QUESTIONS

Group leader, read the following questions and prompts out loud and lead the discussion.

1. More costly and devastating than identity theft in our natural lives is spiritual identity theft, when Satan tries to distort our individual God-given design. Does that statement resonate with you? Have you experienced this threat? If so, in what way(s)?

    Why do you think this is a major tactic of the enemy?

2. Have a volunteer read this definition of Replacement Theology:

    Replacement Theology is the belief that because of Israel's sin, God has withdrawn her unique role as a servant nation. The Jewish people have forfeited their special role in God's redemptive plan. The promises given to Israel in the Old Testament now find their fulfillment through the Church.

    Prior to this lesson, were you aware of this belief? If so, what are your thoughts about it?

3. Which of these statements, if any, have you heard?

    a. The Church is the new Israel.
    b. Christians are spiritual Jews.
    c. God rejected Israel and chose the Church.
    d. The Church will inherit all the promises in the Old Testament, but the curses remain with the Jewish people.
    e. Jewish suffering over the millennia confirms that God has rejected them.

    If one or more of these statements resonate, you may have a Replacement Theology mindset.

4. If God rejected Israel or withdrew their divine calling as His servant for His purposes because of sin, what would stop Him from doing the same to Christians?

Said another way: If God broke the Abrahamic covenant, which He said was everlasting, what would stop Him from breaking the new covenant? Will He?

    a.   Read Hebrews 6:13. What did God use to confirm His covenant with Abraham?

    b.   Read Titus 3:5. What is our salvation based on?

5.   In Jeremiah 31:31–37 God promised the new covenant of our salvation. Does God intend to abandon or cast off national Israel? What is the sign of God's faithfulness to Israel, the sons of Jacob?

6.   Read Jeremiah 33:23–26. What were the people saying? What "I will" promise did God give in verse 26?

7.   Read Leviticus 26:43–45. Will God reject Israel?

> *Will you reject what God has called beloved?*

CONCLUSION

The dangerous doctrine of Replacement Theology brought profound damage to the Jewish community and to the health of the Church. The distortion of identities caused division in the Church, confusion of roles, and a misrepresentation of God's character. It has been a weapon in Satan's hand to thwart the good and holy purposes of God. Sadly, the doctrine is still alive in many seminaries and churches; however, we're living in a day when God is awakening His Church to a correct understanding of Israel.

More formidable than Satan's relentless efforts to divide is God's willingness and all-powerful ability to restore. He calls us to partner with Him to pursue, overtake, and recover all.

God has not rejected Israel from their calling but will keep His covenant with them. The fixed order of day and night—the sun's rising and setting—the expanse of the heavens, and the foundations of the earth are His witnesses.

CLOSE IN PRAYER

As you close your group's time together, see if anyone needs prayer, and take a few minutes to cover those requests.

Ask the Holy Spirit to identify any mistaken identities in your life. Where has the enemy tried to distort God's design for individuals in your group?

Ask the Lord to identify any evidence of Replacement Theology.

PERSONAL STUDY BETWEEN SESSIONS

This section is designed for your personal study to help you dig deeper into some of the themes from the teaching and discussion.

DAY 1

ISRAEL'S TRUE IDENTITY

A primary aim of this course is for us to see Israel through the Father's eyes. There's been an abundance of confusion over Israel's identity because of Replacement Theology, also known as "supersessionism." A tandem blessing to understanding Israel is seeing the Church's true identity. Both are significant to the Father and should be to us as well.

For some, today's Personal Study portion may be a review. For others, it may clarify some fuzzy concepts and affect how they think and speak about Replacement Theology.

Let's address Israel's identity and then look briefly at the Church's.

ISRAEL

- Abraham's family and homeland are eternal provisions guaranteed within the Abrahamic covenant (Gen. 12, 15, 17).
- Abraham's natural descendants, through Isaac and Jacob, are the Jewish people, or Israel. A "seed," the greatest promised Son through Abraham, would be the Messiah (Gen. 35:10–12; 22:18; Gal. 3:16).

- God also promised Abraham spiritual children, from the Gentile nations, who would be joined to Abraham through their individual faith in Jesus, through the new covenant (Gen. 17:4–6; Isa. 56:6–8).

- God chose Israel to be His special treasure, a vessel of purpose, as a servant and witness of God to all people. Their chosen status, however, never guaranteed personal salvation, which only comes through faith in Jesus (Deut. 7:6–7; 26:18).

- In both Testaments, some of Israel believed in the Messiah as Abraham had done, and others did not. The believers are known as the "remnant" and the "Israel within Israel" (Rom. 11:5; 9:27).

- Unbelief in the Messiah didn't disqualify the natural sons of Abraham from being part of the natural family, but it did disqualify them from inclusion in the remnant of believers (John 8:39–47).

In the illustration below, (A) represents Abraham's natural family, the Jewish people. Within that natural family are those without faith (B), or the "unsaved," and those of faith (C), or the "remnant" through faith in the Messiah.

The right side of the illustration (D) represents all Gentiles. Like natural Israel, some Gentiles are of faith (E), "believers," while many are without faith (F), or "unsaved."

Gentiles who come to faith in Jesus through the new covenant are grafted into Abraham's family of faith (Jewish believers, or "the remnant") as spiritual children. The union of believing Jews and Gentiles is the Church (G).

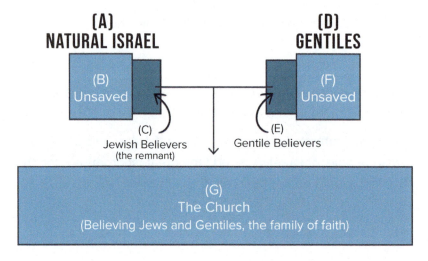

THE CHURCH

What do we learn about the Church in the verses below?

1. Read Ephesians 2:11–22. How is the union of believing Jews and Gentiles described? What various terms did Paul use to describe the new entity?

2. Read Ephesians 3:4–6, 11. How did Paul identify the "mystery of Christ"? According to verse 11, how long has this been God's plan?

What a beautiful eternal plan of God to reach all nations with the gospel! Gentile believers have been grafted into the divine calling given to the Jews to be witnesses of the Lord to all people, make disciples in all nations, and prepare for the Lord's return.

3. Read John 17:17–23. What is the result when the disciples of Jesus—Jewish and Gentile believers, the Church—are unified?

   How is unity described in Psalm 133:1–3, and what will the Lord command in that relational atmosphere?

Replacement Theology has been a weapon in the enemy's hand to disrupt unity within the body of Messiah. Many early Church Gentile fathers didn't just reject unsaved Israel but even the believing remnant—all Israel. The condemnatory accusations were charged to the Jewish soul, at Jewish people as a whole. Not long after the Church was born, Jewish believers were forced to renounce their Jewish heritage as if it were a sin. As Jewish people were scattered throughout the nations and Abraham's land was occupied by others, it was easy to believe God had indeed cast off Israel as a chosen instrument. The Church erred in thinking God's judgment of Israel was permanent. It's God's choice of Israel, God's choosing, that is permanent!

Perhaps the greatest modern miracle happened in 1948 when Israel became a sovereign nation again on her ancient homeland, with Hebrew as a resurrected mother tongue.

Did the Church replace natural, ethnic Israel as the chosen people? Is natural Israel no longer a witness to the world that God exists and that He is faithful to His word? Has God rejected them?

4. Read Ezekiel 39:7, 21–27.

    a. Speaking of an end-times scenario, what did Ezekiel prophesy? Where will God set His name, and who will come to know Him through it? What name of the Lord will be revealed to the nations? (v. 7)

    _____

    _____

    b. Summarize what the nations will know and what will bring the revelation. Will Israel be a witness of God in her righteousness only or even through her iniquity? (vv. 21–27)

    _____

    _____

5. Read Romans 11:1, 11, 28–29 and Isaiah 54:7–8.

a. Writing about natural Israel, what question did Paul ask in Romans 11:1, 11? What was the answer?

b. What do you learn about Israel and God in Romans 11:28–29?

c. What do you learn about Israel and God in Isaiah 54:7–8?

REFLECTION

Has God rejected the natural descendants of Abraham—the Jewish people as a whole? Are they no longer chosen for the purpose of being a witness of God to the world? Has the Church become the new Israel?

In your own words, how would you answer these questions? It's important. How might this truth impact your thoughts toward and interaction with Jewish people in your sphere of influence? How about toward the nation of Israel? Is there an action step you sense the Lord presenting to you?

Abraham's family is God's family. There is one family of faith with distinction among the family members. The Jewish family remains Jewish, and the Gentiles remain Gentile.

FURTHER STUDY

To learn more about Replacement Theology, scan this QR code to read Dr. Wayne Hilsden's article, "Replacement Theology: What Is Supersessionism?"

DAY 2

HOW ARE THE OLD TESTAMENT PROMISES TO BE APPLIED?

Are the promises for the Church? Are they for natural Israel?

1. Read the following verses about the Old Testament Scriptures and write out who they are for and their intended purpose.

    a. Romans 15:4

    _____

    _____

    b. 1 Corinthians 10:11

    _____

    _____

    c. 2 Timothy 3:16–17

    _____

    _____

The whole Bible is for the whole Church—all believers, Jewish and Gentile—and remains applicable to natural Israel. As the apostle Paul studied the Old Testament (Hebrew Scriptures) and God gave him revelation, Paul saw the truth that the "mystery of Christ"—the family of faith includes the Gentiles—was spoken of beginning with Moses and throughout the prophets.

2. Read Romans 15:8–12 and answer the following questions.

   a. verse 8: To whom did Christ become a servant and why?

   _____

   _____

   b. verse 9: Who else did Christ serve and why?

   _____

   _____

   c. verse 10: Paul quoted Moses in Deuteronomy 32:43. The Gentiles are called to rejoice. With whom?

   _____

   _____

Rejoice *with* His people—not *in place* of His people but alongside them, a family of faith. Note that there remains a distinction between the Gentiles and Israel.

The Scriptures were written with us in mind, and we're part of the story. They were written for our use, for our edification and cleansing. The Word of God, the Word made flesh—Jesus (John 1:14)—is for all.

The Scriptures are still for natural Israel. Just as Israel's formation and the prophesied years of chastisement and sorrow have been literal, the promises and prophecies of

Israel's restoration will be literal too. Promises remain for natural Israel. Let's be sure to leave those in place and partner with the Lord in praying and believing for the salvation of Israel—for their full restoration.

REFLECTION

The Song of Solomon is the "Song of Songs" (Song of Sol. 1:1). In other words, it's the highest, the supreme song ever written. There isn't a higher love song.

- Is it written to Solomon's wife, Shulamite, of their marital love?
- Is it a song from God's heart to Israel? Isaiah records that Israel is God's wife.
- Is the song speaking of Jesus and His Church? Paul wrote that we are His bride.
- Is it a song written from the Lord's heart to you?

How about yes and amen to each option? Only God can write something so profound and timeless that it is specific to an individual, true for a nation, and applicable to an international family of faith.

In the song, the bridegroom set his affection upon an unlikely candidate. The bride had been mistreated by others and didn't see herself as special or lovely, but he saw something different. He would walk with her over the years, in every season of their relationship—the highs and the lows—and she would be transformed by his love.

3. Read Song of Solomon 7:10 and write out what the bride comes to be confident in. How does this speak to you? Do you know this for yourself?

_____

_____

4. The choir sings of the bride in Song of Solomon 8:5a. Where is she coming from? What is her posture in the days of her maturity? What does it tell you about her?

_____

_____

How would you describe your posture with the Lord today compared to the bride's?

5. What did Solomon instruct her to do in Song of Solomon 8:6–7? How did he describe his love?

The bride matures to the point of having a vineyard of her own that she's eager for her bridegroom to see. She's been fruitful, and a harvest awaits.

6. Read Song of Solomon 8:14 and Revelation 22:17, 20. What is the bride's call in these verses? Could it be the same call in both Scriptures? How does Jesus reply in Revelation 22:20?

The whole Bible is for the whole Church, and it remains equally applicable and promising for natural Israel, who will one day be awakened to His love. Come, Lord Jesus.

FURTHER STUDY

To learn more about God's love, scan this QR code to read Estera Wieja's article, "'Love What God Loves': What Does It Mean?"

DAY 3
WHAT IS YOUR NAME?

What an interesting question for the Lord to ask Jacob. Of course it wasn't for lack of knowledge. The Lord touched a tender place in Jacob—his identity.

Jacob had fled from Beersheva twenty years earlier. On the way, the Lord appeared to him at Bethel and entrusted to him the Abrahamic covenant promises that had belonged to his father, Isaac, and grandfather, Abraham. In Genesis 28:15, the Lord promised to be with Jacob, to keep him wherever he went, and to bring him back to the land promised in the covenant.

> *Rejoice, O Gentiles, with His people . . . Praise the Lord all you Gentiles, and let all the peoples praise Him. (Rom. 15:10–11)*

Twenty years and a lot of drama had passed. Jacob returned to the land of his inheritance as a wealthy man, with a full family, and in fear of his twin brother, Esau.

Let's pick up this encounter with the Lord. The passage says "a man" wrestled with Jacob, and Jacob said he saw God face-to-face. Hosea 12:4–5 tells us it was an angel, the Lord. There is only one God/Man also known as the Angel of the Lord in the Old Testament, and it's the preincarnate Messiah, Jesus.

1. Read Genesis 32:22–30. What did the Lord change Jacob's name to and for what reason?

The name "Israel" means "he (who) struggles with God" or "God prevails." There is no contradiction here; both understandings of the name have been and still are true. Has Israel struggled with God throughout the millennia? Yes. Has God prevailed on Israel's behalf? *Indeed. And it will continue to be so.*

2. How about you? What is your name? Who has God created you to be? What is your God-given identity?

The One who formed you is the One who gets to identify you. No one else. The Lord fashioned you and gave you natural talents and abilities amid the exquisite details written into your DNA. What a miracle you are.

3. Read Psalm 139 (the entire chapter, if time allows; otherwise, verses 1–6, 13–18). What is your response to these truths?

David called God's works "wonderful" in verse 14 and added, "My soul knows it very well." Your soul encompasses your mind, will, and emotions. Does your soul know it well that God's workmanship of you is wonderful? If not, what hindrances are in the way? Are they based in truth?

In addition to our natural abilities, God has entrusted every believer with supernatural abilities called spiritual gifts to enable us to accomplish our God-given calling. We can't leave home without our spiritual gift(s), and by no means should we consider swapping them for someone else's. God has designed us uniquely and perfectly. Our natural gifts and spiritual gifts fit together and are exactly what we need for what He's called each of us to do.

4. Read 1 Corinthians 12:1, 4–7. What pattern does Paul present in verses 4–6?

___

___

    a. What things does Paul identify as differing?

___

    b. What does he identify as the same?

___

    c. For whose benefit are your giftings, according to verse 7?

___

If you've never studied spiritual gifts, we encourage you to dig further into it. Read 1 Corinthians 12 and Romans 12 for more.

5. Read Ephesians 2:10. What are we called, and for what purpose? When were these prepared for us?

___

___

6. What truths do you read in Philippians 1:6 and 2:13?

　

7. What can we be assured of in Romans 8:28?

　

We can't pretend to be someone we're not. Neither can we reject who God has made us to be and expect to be fulfilled, at peace, or even happy. You were fashioned by God, on purpose, with a purpose, and it's critical to connect with that and go full steam ahead. Jesus said, "I must be about my Father's business" (Luke 2:49 KJV). It's true for each of us!

REFLECTION

8. What do you believe God has called you to in His kingdom? Write it out. If you're not 100 percent sure, that's okay. Take time to pray about it now and write down anything you hear as you listen to the Holy Spirit.

9. Read the *In Essence* lesson summary provided at the beginning of Lesson 4. As you have considered this topic of Replacement Theology and the importance of maintaining a true, God-given identity, have further questions come to mind? Or perhaps you've experienced poignant moments where some dots were connected. If so, write them out.

_____

_____

_____

_____

_____

Replacement Theology has been a two-pronged weapon distorting the identities of Israel and the Church with much pain and confusion, and as a result, division. Let's be rightly aligned to see Israel and the Church through the Father's eyes.

FURTHER STUDY

To learn more about Israel's name and identity, scan this QR code to read Doug Hershey's article, "What Does Israel Mean? Exploring This Important Biblical Name."

I AM GOD, AND THERE IS NO OTHER; I AM GOD, AND THERE IS NO ONE LIKE ME, DECLARING THE END FROM THE BEGINNING, AND FROM ANCIENT TIMES THINGS WHICH HAVE NOT BEEN DONE, SAYING, "MY PURPOSE WILL BE ESTABLISHED, AND I WILL ACCOMPLISH ALL MY GOOD PLEASURE."
(ISA. 46:9–10)

LESSON 5
ISN'T HE OBVIOUS? WHY IT'S DIFFICULT FOR JEWISH PEOPLE TO SEE JESUS

IN ESSENCE

Jesus's identity is not obvious to the Jewish people. Divine and satanic strategies have partially and temporarily hidden God and the gospel message.

Satan has used antisemitism within the Church to persecute Jews, marring Jesus's image and historically presenting a negative testimony of His love to the Jewish community.

God has partially and temporarily hardened the hearts of the Jewish people to the gospel, a divine mystery that has veiled their recognition of Jesus as Messiah. This hiddenness is not entire nor permanent, and one day, the veil will be lifted from Israel's eyes, revealing God's face again.

Believers are called to partner with God in prayer and witness to make the Messiah irresistibly attractive to the Jewish people, anticipating the day when the veil will be lifted, and God's countenance and grace will fully shine upon them.

GETTING STARTED

Group leader, read the In Essence *summary as you begin your time together. This will help set up the direction for this lesson.*

As you open the group time, give everyone an opportunity to answer this question:

▶ What is the first thing that comes to mind when you think about God?

Our experiences play a significant role in how we see the Lord. Attributes of His that are prominent for one person may differ for someone else. How have Israel's experiences affected the way most Jewish people see Jesus? We'll consider that in this week's lesson.

▷ LESSON 5 VIDEO

Group leader, stream the video lesson using the QR code on page 3.

As you watch the video teaching, use the following prompts and space provided to record anything that stands out to you.

1. Jesus should be obvious, right?

2. Satan's role

3. God has been hiding His face from Israel and has caused a partial and temporary hardening of the Jewish heart to the gospel.

4. Isaiah wrote about the effects of the hiddenness, describing Israel as a people who have ears but can't hear, eyes but can't see.

5. Jesus, who perfectly reflects the face of the Father, was partially hidden.

6. God has kept a remnant of Jewish believers. The divine hardening is partial and temporary and in no way entire and permanent.

7. Zechariah wrote of a coming day—a time of an existential threat for Jerusalem—when the Lord will fight on Israel's behalf, and His identity will be revealed.

8. When we see the divine mystery involved here and recognize the forces working against the Jewish people, it should silence criticism and indifference and compel us to action.

GROUP DISCUSSION QUESTIONS

Group leader, read the following questions and prompts out loud and lead the discussion.

1. Before this lesson, did you think Jesus's identity as the Messiah should be obvious to Jewish people? If so, based on what reasons?

2. The Joshua Project reports in 2024 that 95 percent of the worldwide Jewish population hasn't heard the gospel.[1] Why do you think efforts to share the gospel with the Jewish people have been widely nonexistent?

In this week's discussion, we will primarily discuss God's hidden face, a widely unknown factor to most Christians, as one reason it's difficult for Jewish people to see Jesus.

3. Read Deuteronomy 31:14–18. This is not a conditional "If . . . then" statement but a prophecy. What did God reveal Israel would do in the promised land?

   Read Isaiah 59:2. What caused the hiding of God's face?

4. What do you think about the Lord's response of hiding His face from His people?

5. Through Isaiah, God speaks repeatedly of "My servant." Sometimes the reference speaks of the people of Israel, and other times, "My servant" is referring to the Messiah—the perfect servant from Israel. Isaiah 49:1–13 is one of the four "Servant Song" passages foretelling of Jesus. In verse 2, how is the Messiah described?

6. Although Jesus is the exact representation of the Father, His identity was partially hidden when He ministered on earth. Read Matthew 13:10–15 and discuss why Jesus taught in parables to the larger crowds.

   Verses 14–15 show us the effect of the hidden face of God. These verses quote Isaiah 6:9–10. How did Matthew describe the Jewish people in the crowds?

7. Read Isaiah 64:5–12. Discuss how Israel is described in this passage. What are their questions in verses 5 and 12? Has the hidden face reality been a strict punishment?

8. What do we learn about God's discipline of true sons and daughters in Hebrews 12:5–11? How would you want to be treated by other believers during a season of divine discipline? What would you want people to remember about you and about the grace of God?

How can understanding the hidden face of God affect your thinking toward and interactions with Jewish friends and family?

CONCLUSION

Jesus's identity as the Messiah is not obvious to the Jewish community today for several reasons, including God's hidden face. The partial and temporary hardening of the Jewish heart and mind to the truth of the gospel will one day be removed, by the grace of God. Until that great day, may we have compassionate hearts toward Israel, God's firstborn son (Ex. 4:22—23), as the Jewish people undergo a discipline not designed to destroy but to bring them to righteousness.

> *In that day a fountain will be opened for the house of David and for the inhabitants of Jerusalem, for sin and for impurity. (Zech. 13:1)*

> *"I will not hide My face from them any longer, for I will have poured out My Spirit on the house of Israel," declares the Lord GOD. (Ezek. 39:29)*

CLOSE IN PRAYER

As you close your group's time together, see if anyone needs prayer, and take a few minutes to cover those requests.

Pray that the spiritual veil covering the mind and heart of each Jewish person will be taken away (2 Cor. 3:14–16).

Pray for a greater level of love and compassion within the Church to prioritize sharing the gospel of Jesus with the Jewish community.

> *"For a brief moment I forsook you, but with great compassion I will gather you. In an outburst of anger I hid My face from you for a moment, but with everlasting lovingkindness I will have compassion on you," says the LORD your Redeemer. (Isa. 54:7–8)*

PERSONAL STUDY BETWEEN SESSIONS

This section is designed for your personal study to help you dig deeper into some of the themes from the teaching and discussion.

DAY 1

THE SOVEREIGNTY OF GOD

One of God's names is *El Elyon* (אֵל עֶלְיוֹן), "God Most High." It's here we learn that God is sovereign and rules over all.

- Where do you turn when the past is overwhelming?
- Where do you run when there seems to be no way forward?
- Whose embrace is there when the wounds that pierce your heart are from someone trusted?
- Who will have an answer when evil seems to flourish and nothing makes sense?

His name is El Elyon.

In this lesson, we considered hindrances the Jewish people have had in seeing Jesus as their Messiah. We're not surprised by Satan's influences, but God hiding His face from His people—*what do we do with that?*

Maybe you've experienced times that felt beyond what seemed fair, well past the threshold of pain. None of it made sense. The cards seemed stacked against you. Were you without help—or perhaps even hope?

Is there an answer, a strong tower, we can run to and find help and peace?

What does the Bible say about El Elyon—God Most High? Read the verses below and write out what you learn.

1. Daniel 4:34–35: After seven years of insanity and being stripped of his authority and dignity, King Nebuchadnezzar was radically humbled and wrote this about El Elyon.

> *"I will not hide My face from them any longer, for I will have poured out My Spirit on the house of Israel," declares the Lord GOD. (Ezek. 39:29)*

2. Psalm 9:2–4, 9–10

3. Psalm 18:4–19

4. Psalm 21:7

5. Luke 1:32: What did Gabriel reveal about Jesus? Whose Son is He?

6. Romans 9:14, 19–21: What do you learn about God's sovereignty/authority?

___

___

> *While it looks like things are out of control, behind the scenes there is a God who hasn't surrendered His authority.*[2]
> —A. W. Tozer

REFLECTION

The sovereignty of God can seem, at times, like the good news and the bad news. In His sovereignty, He has all power and will ensure we make it through to the other side of the trial—yet why did He allow such a thing to begin with?

The answer to the dilemma is simple: bow our knees to Him and rest. He will allow us to speak and hear our cries. He is not harsh. He's also not our equal. Our compassionate God is the eternal King who rules over heaven and earth and the affairs of mankind.

7. Job endured unbelievable pain and loss. Read Job 42:1–6. What did he say about the things he could not understand? What do you learn from Job's example that you can apply to your life?

___

___

___

___

Can you, like Job, declare the things you don't understand "too wonderful to know"? Is there an area of your life that you need to fully surrender, stop wrestling with, and consider it too wonderful? If so, what is that area?

___

___

8. In verse 5, what did Job's trials provide? Have you also found this to be true in your life? If so, in what ways?

9. How can laying hold of the truth of God's sovereignty and His name, El Elyon, God Most High, affect your day-to-day but also troubling times?

> *When you cannot trace God's hand, trust His heart.*

FURTHER STUDY

This week's lesson highlights how both divine and satanic strategies have partially and temporarily hidden God and the gospel message from the Jewish people.

The lesson primarily emphasizes God's sovereignty in hiding His face from the Jewish people. However, we cannot omit the influence of man's free will and fierce demonic strategies, which have hindered the Jewish people from recognizing Jesus as the Jewish Messiah.

The *In Essence* summary at the beginning of this lesson notes that "Satan has used antisemitism within the Church to persecute Jews, marring Jesus's image and historically presenting a negative testimony of His love to the Jewish community."

Sadly, the ancient hatred of antisemitism is still alive and increasingly prevalent in our day. In response, our team created a miniseries specifically to address this critical issue.

For this week's *Further Study* recommendation, we've included some bonus material for you to consider at your own pace. Scan the QR code below to check out the four-part video series: *Uprooting an Ancient Hatred: What You Need to Know About Antisemitism*. You can watch the videos on FIRM's YouTube channel at your convenience. Visit www.firmisrael.org/hate to download the full PDF notes for the miniseries.

We know there's a lot of content here, but the topic is simply too important to leave out! So if time doesn't permit now, save the videos and watch them later.

DAY 2
GOD'S MYSTERIES

The hidden face of God, the partial hardening of Israel, the Gentiles included in the family of faith . . . the Bible tells us these are divine mysteries.

> *For I do not want you, brethren, to be uniformed of this mystery—so that you will not be wise in your own estimation—that a partial hardening has happened to Israel until the fullness of the Gentiles has come in. (Rom. 11:25)*

In the Greek, the word for "mystery" is *mysterion* (μυστήριον), meaning "a divine secret." It carries the idea of an undiscoverable truth long hidden but made manifest at God's choosing. It's a sovereign El Elyon who reveals His truth when and to whom He chooses.

Paul wrote that we are not to be uniformed. Other translations say, "Don't be ignorant" about truth now revealed. Now that the mysteries are revealed, we're not to live like we're unaware of them. According to the verse above, being ignorant of God's mystery concerning Israel's partial hardening can lead to being wise in our own eyes—in one word, pride.

The Old Testament doesn't speak much about mysteries because that's where they are hidden—in the writings of the ancient prophets and psalmists. Daniel and Job reveal who the keeper and ultimate authority is of the hidden things.

1. Read Job 12:22 and Daniel 2:22 and write out what the authors said of God.

> *There is a God in heaven who reveals mysteries. (Dan. 2:28)*

The New Testament mentions several divine mysteries—truths now revealed by God that had been hidden in shadow form for ages. Below are some.

2. Read these passages and note what mystery is mentioned.

   a. Matthew 13:10–11

   b. Ephesians 1:9

   c. Ephesians 3:4–6

   d. Ephesians 5:31–32

   e. Colossians 1:25–27; 2:2–3

   f. 2 Thessalonians 2:7

God's purposes and plans, His kingdom, the Messiah, and His Church—even the opposition of evil in the last days—are divine mysteries now revealed. Alongside these supreme themes is the mystery of Israel's partial and temporary hardening to the gospel and of seeing God's face.

So why would God cause the partial hardening to Israel? In the Song of Moses, Deuteronomy 32, Moses recorded Israel's history and their future.

> *If we miss understanding what God is doing with Israel, we will miss the full story of God's plan and purposes, and Paul warned we'll become wise in our own eyes.*

3. Read the following verses in Deuteronomy 32 and answer the questions.

   a. verses 9–11: How is God's relationship with Israel described?

   _____

   _____

   b. verses 15–18: What became of Israel (Jeshurun) over time?

   _____

   _____

   c. verses 19–21: What would God do in response?

   _____

   _____

In verse 21 God said He would make Israel jealous with those who are not a people, meaning the Gentiles.

4. Compare this to Romans 10:19–20 and 11:11.

LESSON 5: ISN'T HE OBVIOUS? 107

Interesting, isn't it? God has used the Gentiles and their coming to faith to provoke the Jews to jealousy—to want what Gentile believers have in Messiah.

By Israel's partial hardening, the gospel has come to the Gentiles (Rom. 11:11), but it is not to stop there—it is to circle back to Israel again. Will you be part of that God-given purpose? Will you see Israel through the Father's eyes and love what He loves?

In Deuteronomy 32:36, Moses wrote: "For the LORD will vindicate His people, and will have compassion on His servants."

5. Read Deuteronomy 32:43. Who is to rejoice and why? What does this tell us is coming for ethnic Israel?

___

___

___

REFLECTION

But You are a God of forgiveness, gracious and compassionate, slow to anger and abounding in mercy; and You did not abandon them. (Neh. 9:17 NASB)

We've looked at some divine mysteries revealed in the Bible, but we've each had personal mysteries in our lives—things we've experienced or seen that have left us baffled and wondering, *Lord, what are You doing? Why?*

Is there an answer for those mysteries in our lives? Remember that God is El Elyon. He's sovereign, He rules over all, and He's a loving Father. If we need to know—if we can handle the answer—He'll tell us.

6. What does He promise in Jeremiah 33:3?

___

___

7. What do you learn about the Lord's wisdom and ways in Isaiah 55:8–9?

The distance between the earth and the sun is 93 million miles. God's wisdom reaches far beyond that measurement, but just think of that distance: Would it be reasonable to believe that the answers to the mysteries and unexplained dilemmas we've experienced are (figuratively) tucked into the 93 million miles of His wisdom that is beyond us? There are answers to the unexplained, and you never know when El Elyon will see fit, in His measureless wisdom, to reach into the 93 million miles, grab hold of the exact revelation or answer you need, and make it known.

Until then, remember Job's words in Job 42:3 and *consider the things you don't understand too wonderful for you to know.*

8. Considering God's sovereignty from Day 1, His mystery and unmatched wisdom, how would you counsel yourself in an area of need today?

DAY 3
GOD'S HIDDEN FACE REVEALED IN JOSEPH'S STORY

Genesis records the story of Jacob's beloved son, Joseph, who was sold into slavery in Egypt by his jealous brothers. After years of struggle, through a series of miraculous events and God's faithfulness, Joseph was suddenly thrust into power—second only to Pharaoh.

During Joseph's years of obscurity, Jacob remained in Canaan with his other sons and their families, including Joseph's youngest and only full brother, Benjamin. Based on a lie, Jacob believed Joseph had been killed. In a time of severe famine, Jacob sent his sons, except Benjamin, to Egypt to purchase food. Who would they encounter, but the brother they had betrayed.

Joseph recognized his brothers immediately, but they could not discern his identity—his face was hidden to them because of the Egyptian context. They had no idea the lord of the land was their brother, Joseph.

Joseph had his brothers present themselves before him. In the first instance, Joseph kept his identity hidden and tested them. He gave them grain but required them to bring Benjamin to him. For collateral, Joseph kept Simeon (whose name means "hearing") in prison until the brothers returned with Benjamin (Gen. 42).

These events in Genesis literally happened, but the story also points to a spiritual truth, a prophetic picture. In the same way his brothers couldn't "see" Joseph, who foreshadows Jesus, most Jewish people didn't recognize Jesus's true identity as Messiah at His first coming. Simeon (or "hearing") was locked up (literally, in the Joseph story), but we see the prophetic truth carried into the present as well. Think of Isaiah's words: *My people cannot see or hear the truth* (Isa. 6:10). Jesus quoted Isaiah to say the same was true about the people in His generation (Mark 4:12).

1. Read Genesis 43:1–5. What did Judah report that "the man" had warned the brothers?

   _____

   _____

2. Read Genesis 43:13–14. What did Jacob hope his sons would receive from God and for what purpose? Remember the meaning of Simeon's name.

   _____

   _____

Joseph's servants brought the brothers before him two more times (Gen. 43–44).

> *It will be God's compassion that unlocks "hearing" from its prison; His compassion will open the eyes and ears of the Jewish people again to His face and His voice.*

3. Read Genesis 45:1–7. Again, this literally happened, but don't miss the spiritual picture. Joseph is a type or foreshadow of Jesus, whose hidden face will one day be revealed to His own family. What stands out to you about Joseph's unveiling and encounter with his brothers?

   _____

   _____

4. Joseph saw the larger purpose for all he had endured. In verses 5 and 7, what did he recognize as the reason for his suffering? The same idea is expressed in Genesis 50:20.

   _____

   _____

LESSON 5: ISN'T HE OBVIOUS?

How is that same picture true of Jesus's life and ministry?

One day, this story will have its prophetic fulfillment when Jesus returns to earth and the veil and partial hardening currently over the Jewish heart and mind will be removed. The Lord will return one day for an entire family of faith, but all the "brothers" must be present—including Benjamin, Joseph's full brother, or the Jewish people, prophetically.

God revealed through the prophet Zechariah what that day will be like when Jesus returns and His face is unveiled before His brethren. It will be a severe day, in a time when Jerusalem is under attack. Jesus, who came first as the Lamb of God, will return as a warring king.

5. Read Zechariah 12:1–3, 8–10; 13:1, 6.

Until the day Zechariah prophesied, the veil can be lifted through faith in Jesus, one individual at a time. Will you pray for the compassion of God to be upon the Jewish people today to see Jesus? It's God's heart for all people, from every nation, to know Him.

The Bible is clear: the world will be in an extremely critical time when Jesus returns. Paul presented Timothy with a description of the last days in 2 Timothy 3:1–7.

In the Joseph story, the context is a severe famine that covered the earth.

> *Seek the LORD while He may be found; call upon Him while He is near. (Isa. 55:6)*

6. In Amos 8:11, how does Amos describe the famine that will come? Does it seem possible that our culture, even the world, could be heading toward that scenario, or in it now?

REFLECTION

The last days will be severe and there will be a famine of the Word, but it doesn't have to be a famine for you. Even as Joseph prepared the world by storing grain in a time when the grain could be found, so too, now is the time for each of us to feast on the Bread of Life, to fill our own hearts and minds with the very Words of God.

7. What invitation did God give in Isaiah 55:1–3?

8. What promise did Jesus give in Matthew 5:6?

9. How would you describe your sense of hunger and appetite for the Word of God, the Bible? Would you renew your commitment to it? Would you share the Word with those around you? Today is the day of salvation.

> *Open my eyes, that I may behold wonderful things from Your law. (Ps. 119:18)*

10. Read the *In Essence* lesson summary provided at the beginning of Lesson 5. As you have considered why it's difficult for Jewish people to see Jesus, have further questions come to mind? Or perhaps you've experienced poignant moments where some dots were connected. If so, write them out.

Behold, now is "the acceptable time"; behold, now is "the day of salvation" (2 Cor. 6:2).

FURTHER STUDY

To learn more about God's hidden face, scan this QR code to read the article by FIRM staff, "Why Don't Most Jewish People Recognize Jesus?"

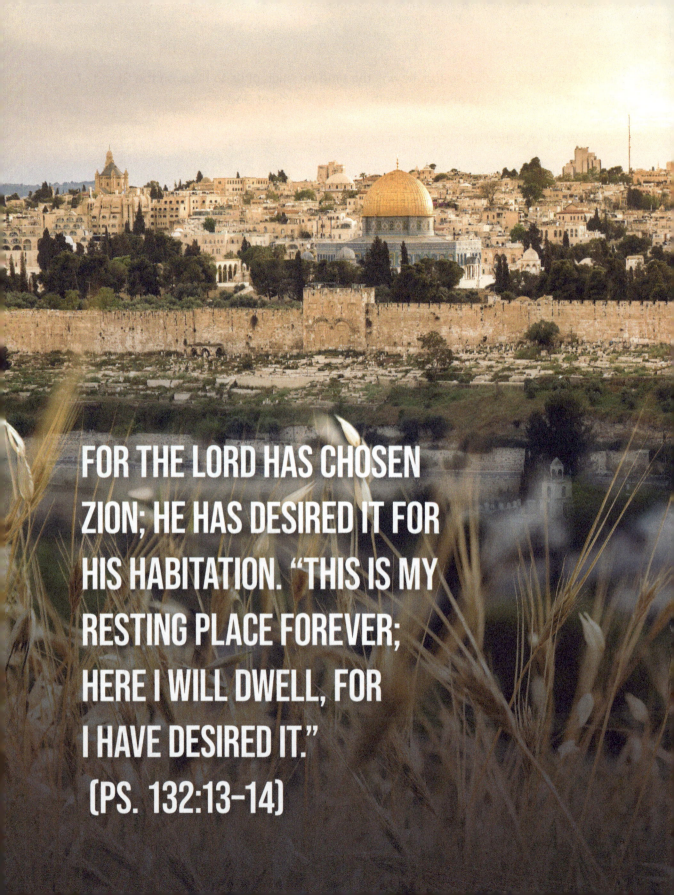

LESSON 6
JERUSALEM, JERUSALEM: THE CITY OF THE GREAT KING

IN ESSENCE

Jerusalem, which means "foundation of peace," is the place where the blood of Jesus purchased our peace. It is the place of God's habitation and where His desire is, where He has written His name, and upon which are His heart and eyes. It will be the place of Jesus's throne when He returns to reign as King. Until that day, a spiritual battle rages over this city. Jerusalem is like a threshing floor, a place of sifting and separation. God has chosen it for Himself, and Satan is leading a rebellion against it, challenging God's authority.

We are invited to partner with God's redemptive plan for this city and its people—to pray for the peace of Jerusalem and declare God's eternal purposes to see His will accomplished on earth as it is in heaven.

GETTING STARTED

Group leader, read the In Essence *summary as you begin your time together. This will help set up the direction for this lesson.*

As you open the group time, give everyone an opportunity to answer this question:

▶ Where is "home" to you, and why is that place significant?

The psalmist recorded that Zion, or Jerusalem, is God's desired place of habitation, His resting place forever (Ps. 132:13–14). What makes Jerusalem significant to God? Should it also be a place of importance to us? Let's find out what the Bible says about Jerusalem in this week's lesson.

▶ LESSON 6 VIDEO

Group leader, stream the video lesson using the QR code on page 3.

As you watch the video teaching, use the following prompts and space provided to record anything that stands out to you.

1. "Jerusalem" means "foundation of peace."

   _____

   _____

2. Jerusalem is at the center of God's heart. Why?

   _____

   _____

3. When Jesus returns, Jerusalem will again be like a threshing floor, a place of separation, where the righteous and unrighteous will be separated.

   _____

   _____

4. Satan was determined to have God's place, His throne of authority, and the worship that belongs to God alone.

   _____

   _____

5. Satan wants what he has always wanted: place and worship. He wants these in the spiritual realm, on earth, and in our lives.

   _____

   _____

6. Satan has continually sought to occupy, corrupt, and destroy the city God calls His own.

7. Pray for the peace of Jerusalem.

> *God has called us to partner with Him in His eternal purposes.*
>
> *Thus the LORD was moved by prayer for the land. (2 Sam. 24:25)*

GROUP DISCUSSION QUESTIONS

Group leader, read the following questions and prompts out loud and lead the discussion.

1. In the Old Testament, names are significant in identifying character and purpose. "Jerusalem" means "foundation of peace." From your perspective, how does Jerusalem's modern context align with its name?

2. Moses wrote Deuteronomy as Israel prepared to cross into the promised land. What instruction did God give Israel in Deuteronomy 12:10–14? Watch for the words "the place" and "there."

    a. Who chose the "place," and why was it chosen? (v. 11)

    b. Could the children of Israel fulfill their sacrificial requirements anywhere they wanted?

3. God chose Jerusalem as the place for His name to dwell (2 Chron. 6:6). According to Isaiah 18:7, what name of God is identified as being connected to Mount Zion, which is Jerusalem?

    Note: This name means the "Lord of the armies" or the "heavenly hosts." It's a name for times of conflict and warfare.

4. According to 2 Chronicles 3:1, where did Solomon build the temple, and what was the site used for before King David purchased it?

    a. According to 2 Chronicles 7:12, for what purpose did God choose that place?

    b. According to Isaiah 24:23, what future purpose will it have?

5. Discuss within your group why it's significant that God's choice of place for His name—the place of Jesus's sacrifice and future throne—was a threshing floor. What does it speak to us of?

    Note: In Scripture, threshing floors were a place of separation, where a price was paid, a decision was made (Gideon), a woman met her future husband (Ruth and Boaz), the harvest was gathered, and where the enemy threatened the harvest.

6. Where does the Holy Spirit dwell today, according to 1 Corinthians 3:16 and 6:19–20?

7. Using spiritual imagery, are our lives, in a sense, a threshing floor? Are there areas within our hearts and minds that are places of separation and decision where a price must be paid? How so?

8. Michael said that Satan wants "the place" and "the worship" in natural Jerusalem and in our lives. Can you identify where the enemy is most at work to steal what God has established in you? How about in the culture you live in?

9. The name of God connected to Jerusalem is the Lord of hosts—the Lord of the armies. Why is this significant and how can this name of God impact your circumstances today?

> *The LORD of hosts has sworn saying, "Surely, just as I have intended so it has happened, and just as I have planned so it will stand." (Isa. 14:24)*

CONCLUSION

Jerusalem is like no other city on earth. Even as the Jewish people have been chosen, God chose Jerusalem as the place of His ultimate sacrifice and future throne. It's His city for His purposes. Satan desires every "place" and sound of worship that belongs to God—whether in heaven, on the earth, or in our lives. It's a spiritual battle, and the Lord of hosts will have His way. The gospel will go forth from Jerusalem to every nation, tribe, tongue, and people (Rev. 14:6) before Jesus returns to Jerusalem as King.

> *Pray for the peace of Jerusalem: "May they prosper who love you." (Ps. 122:6)*

> *You who remind the LORD, take no rest for yourselves; and give Him no rest until He establishes and makes Jerusalem a praise in the earth. (Isa. 62:6–7)*

CLOSE IN PRAYER

As you close your group's time together, see if anyone needs prayer, and take a few minutes to cover those requests.

Identify the significant spiritual battles group members are facing and stand with one another in prayer to see the enemy defeated and the Lord magnified.

Pray for physical and spiritual peace of Jerusalem, protection for the people and city—and for Israel to know the Prince of Peace.

> *Who may ascend the mountain of the LORD? Who may stand in his holy place? The one who has clean hands and a pure heart, who does not trust in an idol or swear by a false god. (Ps. 24:3–4 NIV)*

PERSONAL STUDY BETWEEN SESSIONS

This section is designed for your personal study to help you dig deeper into some of the themes from the teaching and discussion.

DAY 1

MOUNT MORIAH — CHOSEN BY GOD

The land of Israel is arguably the most contested real estate in the world. Let's explore this further. Within Israel, the city of Jerusalem has endured centuries of dispute. Within Jerusalem, the piece of real estate bearing more struggle than any other place is the Temple Mount.

The Temple Mount is considered holy to Jews, Christians, and Muslims, but for different reasons.

Why the uproar over that "place" and the worship that ascends from there? What does the Bible have to say about the location of the Jewish temple?

> Then Solomon began to build the house of the LORD in Jerusalem on Mount Moriah, where the LORD had appeared to his father David, at the place that David had prepared on the threshing floor of Ornan the Jebusite. *(2 Chron. 3:1)*

The word *Moriah* (מוֹרִיָּה) in Hebrew means "chosen by God." *Chosen!* Chosen for what? Like the Jewish people and like Jerusalem, God chose Mount Moriah for a specific reason and purpose.

The first mention of Mount Moriah is in Genesis 22, when God tested Abraham. Let's discover why God chose Mount Moriah for Himself.

1. Read Genesis 22:1–14 and answer the following questions.

   a. verse 2: How is Isaac described, and what instruction did God give Abraham?

   _____

   _____

   b. verse 8: What did Abraham believe about the sacrifice?

   _____

   _____

   c. verse 10: What was Abraham's posture, and what did he have in his hand?

   _____

   _____

   d. verse 11: Who spoke to Abraham?
   Note: Most scholars agree this figure is the preincarnate Jesus.

   _____

   e. verse 14: What did Abraham name that place, the chosen mountain in Moriah?

   _____

> **MORIAH** *in Hebrew means "chosen by God."*
>
> *Abraham called the name of that place The LORD Will Provide. (Gen. 22:14)*

It's in Genesis 22 that the words "love," "obey," and "worship" are first mentioned in the Bible. Sacrifice is the context for these monumental biblical themes.

122 LOVE WHAT GOD LOVES

2. How are the themes of love, obedience, and worship displayed in Genesis 22 through Abraham and Isaac's actions?

___

3. God had faithfully provided for Abraham over the years—but never at a more significant moment than with the ram. What do you imagine went through Abraham's mind?

___

The Genesis 22 account foreshadows another Father greater than Abraham, God the Father, who would not withhold His only Son but offer Him on Mount Moriah. Let's look at the other significant event that took place at this exact location.

In 2 Chronicles 3:3 (above) we learn Mount Moriah was also the place where the Lord appeared to David at the threshing floor. In this biblical scene, the reason for the sacrifice of God's Son is foreshadowed.

The context of this story is that Satan moved King David to call for a census within Israel. This was not to be done; David committed a great sin against the Lord.

4. Read 1 Chronicles 21:7–18, 22–27 and answer the following questions.

a. verse 14: What did God send upon Israel, and what was the cost in lives?

b. verse 16: What posture did the angel of the Lord (the preincarnate Jesus) have, and what was in his hand? How does this compare to Abraham in Genesis 22:10?

c. verses 18, 22: What did David build on the threshing floor and why?

d. verse 24: What was David willing to pay and why?

e. verse 26: Where did the fire (a picture of judgment) come from to consume the burnt offering?

5. Read 1 Chronicles 22:1. What did David call that place, and what would it be used for?

6. The plague was stopped because of David's sacrifice at the threshing floor. According to Hebrews 10:10–12, 14, what "plague" is stopped because of Jesus's sacrifice?

REFLECTION

Sin must be punished. Sin had unsheathed the sword, and without a sin-offering, there was no sheathing it again. "It is enough," the Lord said in 1 Chronicles 21; "It is finished," Jesus said from the cross.

7. "In the mount of the LORD, it will be provided," Abraham prophesied in Genesis 22:14. Is there a sin that entangles you today? If so, what is it? Paul wrote "and do not give the devil an opportunity" in Ephesians 4:27. The Greek word for "opportunity" translates as "place."

Upon Jesus alone, the fire of judgment fell. If you belong to Him, the power of sin has been broken from your life. How can this truth free you from condemnation?

Do you see, friend, why the Temple Mount in Jerusalem today is steeped in a spiritual battle? No wonder Satan wants to rewrite the story in that place and confiscate the worship. The Lord has summoned believers to stand with Him and pray for Jerusalem's peace until the day Jerusalem becomes a praise in the earth (Isa. 62:7). Will you pray?

▷ FURTHER STUDY

To learn more about the biblical site Mount Moriah, scan this QR code to read Doug Hershey's article, "What Is the Temple Mount and Why Is It Important?"

DAY 2
NO GREATER LOVE

The first mention of "love" in the Bible is in Genesis 22:2 in the context of Abraham, a loving father who would not withhold his only son as a sacrifice on Mount Moriah. Here, the grand biblical themes of love and sacrifice are joined, and the two remain connected throughout the entirety of Scripture.

A line from an old, Italian poem states: "Love's strength standeth in Love's sacrifice." [3]

1. What did Jesus declare in John 15:13?

   _____

   _____

2. Besides Jesus's love for you, whose sacrificial love has had the most significant impact on your life? How has it affected you?

   _____

   _____

3. According to Romans 5:7–8, at what point in our lives did Jesus willingly die for us?

   _____

a. How hard or easy is it for you to accept that God loves you unconditionally, even before you loved Him?

_____

_____

b. Are there hindrances to your believing it? If so, what? Ask the Holy Spirit to meet you in the place of doubt or unbelief, heal the wound there, and bring you to a place where you can fully receive His love.

_____

_____

The apostle John wrote about love and love's sacrifice more than any other biblical author.

4. Look up the following verses and write out what you see about love and love's sacrifice.

a. John 3:16 (note who the focus of God's love is)

_____

_____

b. John 10:17–18 (Jesus is speaking)

_____

_____

c. John 13:1, 34

_____

d. 1 John 4:9–11

e. Ephesians 5:1–2

REFLECTION

When did the apostle John receive the revelation that love's greatest expression is found in sacrifice?

On the night of Jesus's arrest, Peter and "another disciple" followed Jesus and entered the high priest's courtyard, where Jesus was falsely accused and beaten. Scholars believe John was referring to himself as the other disciple (John 18:15–16).

Later, John stood nearby the cross at Jesus's crucifixion. Despite a viciously beaten and likely swollen face, Jesus spoke to John and entrusted His mother into John's care. No doubt, John held a trembling, grieving Mary as she looked upon her beloved son, who had been tortured beyond recognition—His appearance marred more than any other man's (Isa. 52:14).

"It is finished!" And He bowed His head and gave up His spirit. (John 19:30)

To expedite matters, the Roman soldiers broke the legs of the two thieves crucified next to the Lord. When they came to Jesus, though, He was already dead. Water and blood gushed from His side as they thrust the spear into his chest cavity. Jesus paid the ultimate price to stop sin's plague of death directed at us.

John added this profound statement in John 19:35:

> *And he who has seen has testified, and his testimony is true; and he knows that he is telling the truth, so that you also may believe.*

In essence, John said this: "I've seen with my own eyes the gore and suffering; I see the price of our sin—my sin. I see the cost of my sin upon Him! My soul is pierced. I'm telling the truth—there has never been a greater sacrifice of love than this. He is the Son of God, our Messiah. I believe—will you?"

> *We know love by this, that He laid down His life for us. (1 John 3:16)*

Five times in John's gospel he refers to himself as "the disciple whom Jesus loved." He's known through history as "John the Beloved," yet not once do we read of Jesus calling him this. It was a personal revelation as John beheld the sacrifice—and he was never the same. Jesus's sacrificial love shaped John's identity.

5. In what ways can unconditional, sacrificial love change how we see ourselves? Has Jesus's love transformed your identity, your view of yourself? If so, how so?

_____

_____

_____

_____

Love's strength standeth in Love's sacrifice. You are so loved! There's no greater love than this.

▶ FURTHER STUDY

To learn more about the Hebrew word for love in the Bible, scan this QR code to read Estera Wieja's article, "Hebrew Word for Love: 4 Biblical & Modern Words to Know."

DAY 3
JERUSALEM WILL BE A PRAISE IN THE EARTH

Michael closed the teaching this week by quoting the Isaiah 62 call to prayer for Zion's sake, for Jerusalem.

> *For Zion's sake I will not keep silent, and for Jerusalem's sake I will not keep quiet, until her righteousness goes forth like brightness, and her salvation like a torch that is burning. . . . You who remind the Lord, take no rest for yourselves; and give Him no rest until He establishes and makes Jerusalem a praise in the earth. (Isa. 62:1, 6–7)*

There are two time-identifiers in these verses, both starting with the word "until." Pray like crazy—*until*:

- Jerusalem's righteousness and salvation shine brightly
- God establishes her (Jerusalem) as a praise in the earth

In other words, there is coming a day when Jerusalem's battles will be over, her inhabitants will all know the Lord, and the world will unanimously erupt in praise at what God has accomplished on Jerusalem's behalf.

Because God has chosen Jerusalem and Mount Moriah as the place for His name, the place of His habitation forever, the place of highest sacrifice, victory, and expression of love, Satan has thrown his entire arsenal at it. Jerusalem has been attacked fifty-two times, captured and recaptured forty-four times, besieged twenty-three times, and destroyed two times. *Oh, Jerusalem! The saints have been summoned to never be silent until your day of restoration.*

When will that be? What will be the setting?

Let's take a cursory look at Jerusalem's future restoration and high calling. There are many perspectives and details surrounding end-times events, and we won't get deep into all that (although it's interesting!), but we can identify general details. As we conclude our lesson about Jerusalem, let's close it by seeing her in her beauty.

1. Look up these verses and write out what you learn about Jerusalem (Zion) and the people.

    a. Micah 4:11–12 speaks of the time prior to Jerusalem's full victory. Note what posture the nations take.

    b. Matthew 23:37–39; Hosea 5:15: What will happen before Jesus's return?

    c. Psalm 2:1–6

d. Zephaniah 3:14–17, 20

e. Jeremiah 32:37–42

f. Isaiah 2:1–4

g. Isaiah 24:23; 25:6–10a

REFLECTION

2. What stands out to you about the Lord as you consider the truths in the verses above?

   _____
   _____
   _____
   _____
   _____
   _____

3. Is there an attribute about Him that you see present in His dealings with Jerusalem, the city and the people, that you need in your life today? What is it? Take some time to pray about that.

   _____
   _____
   _____
   _____
   _____
   _____

In Day 1, we saw in 1 Chronicles 21:15 that when the judgment of pestilence was about to wipe out Jerusalem altogether, the Lord spoke, "It is enough."

In Day 2, in John 19, from the cross that resulted in our salvation, Jesus said, "It is finished!"

Today, as we consider the future of Jerusalem, we read these words from Jesus in Revelation 21:6, "It is done."

The One who will sit on the throne in Jerusalem is making all things new—these words are faithful and true.

Be encouraged today, no matter your circumstances. God is faithful and able! His heart is for you. Even as the Lord of hosts is bringing Jerusalem to her expected end, her prophesied completeness, He will bring you through to yours!

> *How blessed is the man whose strength is in You, in whose heart are the highways to Zion! Passing through the valley of Baca [weeping] they make it a spring . . . they go from strength to strength. (Ps. 84:5–7)*

4. Read the *In Essence* lesson summary provided at the beginning of Lesson 6. As you have considered the topic of Jerusalem, have further questions come to mind? Or perhaps you've experienced poignant moments where some dots were connected. If so, write them out.

_____

_____

_____

_____

> *Jerusalem is like a threshing floor, a place of sifting and separation. God has chosen it for Himself, and Satan is leading a rebellion against it.*

FURTHER STUDY

To learn more about how to effectively pray for Jerusalem, scan this QR code to read Dr. Wayne Hilsden's article, "How to Pray for the Peace of Jerusalem."

THE WILDERNESS AND THE DESERT WILL REJOICE, AND THE DESERT WILL SHOUT FOR JOY AND BLOSSOM . . . THEY WILL SEE THE GLORY OF THE LORD, THE MAJESTY OF OUR GOD.
(ISA. 35:1–2 NASB 2020)

LESSON 7
ISRAEL'S FUTURE HOPE: THE COMING REVIVAL

IN ESSENCE

Hope is central to our stories, because we serve a God of great hope.

The same prophets who prophesied Israel's discipline prophesied her restoration to the land and to the Lord. Israel's natural deliverance and spiritual salvation are intertwined. Difficult days ahead will culminate in the Lord's return. Jesus will destroy His enemies, unveil Israel's eyes to receive Him fully, and present to Himself a spotless bride from every tribe, tongue, and nation. Jerusalem will dwell securely as King Jesus will reign in justice and peace, fulfilling His covenant with David.

There is coming a day that Peter called the "restoration of all things" about which God spoke by the prophets of old (Acts 3:21). God will complete what He has started. He is not done with the Church, He is not done with Israel, and He is not done with us, individually.

GETTING STARTED

Group leader, read the In Essence *summary as you begin your time together. This will help set up the direction for this lesson.*

As you open the group time, give everyone an opportunity to answer this question:

▶ What do you hope to be doing ten years from now?

Thinking about the future may inspire or even unsettle us. The truth is, for Israel and all believers, our futures are anchored in hope. Let's join Kayla and Michael as we look at Israel's future hope and then, throughout the lesson, see how all believers have a shared destiny.

▶ LESSON 7 VIDEO

Group leader, stream the video lesson using the QR code on page 3.

As you watch the video teaching, use the following prompts and space provided to record anything that stands out to you.

1. Israel's return to the land is a predominant theme of prophecy and a witness of God's faithfulness to Abraham.

2. Israel does not yet resemble the glorious picture the prophets painted. We see partial fulfillment.

> *We have been unfaithful to our God . . . yet now there is hope for Israel in spite of this. (Ezra 10:2)*

3. Israel will also experience a restoration to the Lord.

4. Tumultuous days ahead will demand a mighty deliverance for Israel. The realm of war is both natural and spiritual. So will be the realm of victory.

5. This cataclysmic time will bring about both the Lord's return to Israel and Israel's return to the Lord. A key: Matthew 23:39

   _____

   _____

6. Israel will experience a profound awakening, a turning of hearts toward their long-awaited Messiah.

   _____

   _____

7. The Bible emphasizes both heavenly (spiritual) and earthly (natural) dimensions of God's kingdom.

   _____

   _____

8. God's restoration of Israel—to the land, to the Lord, and to usher in the reign of King Jesus—is for the sake of His holy name.

   _____

   _____

9. Israel's future hope gives us great assurance for God's promises to all believers.

   _____

   _____

GROUP DISCUSSION QUESTIONS

Group leader, read the following questions and prompts out loud and lead the discussion.

A working definition of hope is "desire with expectation for a positive future."

1. What are the top two things you are hoping for spiritually?

    On a scale of 1–10 (10 being high), how would you rate your hope of seeing these?

2. What is the believer's hope? After your group discusses possible answers, read the following verses. Would you change any of your answers?

    a. Matthew 12:15, 21
    b. Titus 2:11–13; 3:7
    c. 1 Corinthians 15:19–26

3. The Lord revealed to the Old Testament prophets His plan for salvation, the scope of His reach, and His kingdom reign. Look up the following verses and summarize what is prophesied.

    Hope of the Messiah

    a. Isaiah 53 the "Servant" (see also Isa. 52:13–14)
        - verses 3–5: How is He described?
        - verses 6, 8, 11, 12: What would be placed upon Him?
        - verse 9: Was He guilty?
        - verse 10: Who put Him to death, and would He live again?

    b. Jeremiah 23:5–6; Isaiah 9:6–7: How is the Messiah described here?

    Hope of a Messianic People

    - Isaiah 49:6: Who will His salvation reach?

Hope of a Messianic Kingdom

   a.   Isaiah 2:2–4
   b.   Isaiah 11:6–9

This was Israel's hope: the Lord Himself (Jer. 17:13) and His full purpose and plan for a Savior and restoration of all the prophets had spoken. It's a redemption plan involving Israel and the nations. Some of it has been fulfilled, and some remains. If God has been faithful to the first part, will He be faithful to what remains?

4. Read Acts 26:6, 22–23. What was Paul on trial for?

   Also read Acts 28:20, 23. Why was Paul in chains?

The prophets prophesied Israel's discipline, exile, and restoration. Jesus was the "stone of stumbling," the "rock of offense" that Israel stumbled over and, as a result, fell into a long season of disobedience. Will there be a recovery? Will they see what the prophets foretold?

5. What does the Lord promise in Jeremiah 29:10–14?
6. Is the hope of the believer and the hope of Israel different or the same? Give a reason for your answer.

CONCLUSION

In this course, we want to be stirred to love what God loves and see Israel through the Father's eyes. As we consider the prophetic promises given to Israel, we must ask, *Will the prophecies presently unfulfilled come to pass? Does Israel have a future and a hope in God?* The answer is yes. Regardless of the delay, God will complete what He promised.

That principle is true for Israel, it is true for the Church, and it is true for you.

Israel has been, and is being, restored to her promised land, and one day, when Jesus returns for His own, the veil will be lifted from Israel's eyes, and all that the prophets prophesied, for all nations, will be ushered into fulfillment (Acts 3:20–21).

CLOSE IN PRAYER

As you close your group's time together, see if anyone needs prayer, and take a few minutes to cover those requests.

Pray into the areas where hope is lost or deferred. Take time to encourage one another and to bear one another's burdens.

> *Sing aloud with gladness for Jacob, and raise shouts for the chief of the nations; proclaim, give praise, and say, "O LORD, save your people, the remnant of Israel." (Jer. 31:7 ESV)*

PERSONAL STUDY BETWEEN SESSIONS

This section is designed for your personal study to help you dig deeper into some of the themes from the teaching and discussion.

DAYS 1 & 2

This will be a larger topic than normal for our Personal Study sessions, so feel free to divide your time over two days.

THE COMING REVIVAL

Many times in the Old Testament a prophet would speak of an event or detail that would have a near fulfillment, and in the next breath, reach to the distant future and prophesy of the last days—all in one sentence—keeping us on our toes. There is an "already-and-not-yet" reality in biblical prophecy. Some things have already been fulfilled, and some not yet.

In the lesson this week, Michael spoke of Israel's prophesied restoration to the promised land and their restoration to the Lord. In both areas, "already-and-not-yet" realities are in effect.

Beginning in the late nineteenth century, the Jewish people began to make a concerted, passionate effort to return to their ancient homeland. The miraculous rebirth of Israel as a sovereign state in 1948 is not inconsequential but biblical prophecy being fulfilled. Yet, Israel doesn't currently have sovereignty over all the land promised to Abraham's descendants, so Israel's restoration to the land is "already and not yet." It's partially fulfilled, with more to come.

The same pattern is true for Israel's restoration to the Lord. Every generation has a remnant of Jewish believers faithful to the Lord and looking to the Messiah; however, Scripture does not just promise a remnant of Jewish believers—a day is coming when *all Israel will be saved*. There is an "already-and-not-yet" reality today for the salvation of Israel. Jewish believers are alive and well in Israel and around the world, but there is still a future hope for all Israel alive at the time of Jesus's return.

ISRAEL'S RETURN TO THE LORD

In the first two days of the *Personal Study* this week, we will look at what remains to be fulfilled as we wait in hope for the day when Israel will be restored to the Lord spiritually. This is critical to us as believers because Israel's spiritual restoration will coincide with the fullness of the Gentiles when Abraham's family—natural and spiritual sons and daughters—will all come into their fullness. We have a shared destiny. *It will be a miraculous, glorious time—so let's see it in the Word.*

1. The salvation of Israel is the hope of the prophets. Read these passages and note what you learn.

    a. Jeremiah 31:33–34

    _____

    _____

    _____

    b. Isaiah 59:20–21

    _____

    _____

    _____

c. Zechariah 12:10; 13:1

d. Isaiah 4:2–5

Paul wrote in Romans 8 that nothing can separate us from the love of God (vv. 38–39) and then anticipated the church in Rome's next questions: *What about Israel? As a nation, they rejected Jesus. Have the Jewish people been separated from God?* In Romans 9–11 Paul brilliantly addressed the questions and answered with a resounding, *"May it never be!"* (Rom. 11:1, 11).

> O LORD, the hope of Israel . . . Heal me, O LORD, and I will be healed; save me and I will be saved, for You are my praise. (Jer. 17:13–14)

In Romans 11 Paul wrote of the "fullness" of Israel (v. 12) and the "fullness of the Gentiles" (v. 25).

The word "fullness" in Greek is *pleroma* and means "complete, filled up, and overflowing."

The term was used to speak of a ship *filled* with everything needed for the voyage. It was used of God being *full* of goodness and of Him *filling* all of earth and heaven. There is no shortfall, but everything is in its place, filled to overflowing and complete. A day is coming when Israel and the Gentiles (even all of creation!) will be in a state of God's intended *fullness*.

> *But when the fullness of the time came, God sent forth His Son.*
> *(Gal. 4:4)*

2. Read Romans 11:11–12, 15. Paul was writing about natural Israel—the Jewish people.

   a. As a result of their sin of rejecting Jesus, what came about?

   _____

   _____

   b. What was Paul's line of reason in verse 12?

   _____

   _____

We find Israel's *fullness* spoken of here. If Israel's "failure" led to salvation for the Gentiles, what will happen when Israel's prophesied salvation, their fullness, is realized?

   c. What will Israel's fullness, their acceptance of Jesus, be according to verse 15?

   _____

Life from the dead, in a word, is resurrection. Within the believer's hope we look forward with expectation to a resurrection.

   d. What did Paul teach in 1 Corinthians 15:20–23? When is the resurrection of the dead and who will be raised?

   _____

   _____

   _____

Israel's *fullness*—Israel's salvation, the "all Israel" that is prophesied—is connected to the resurrection of the dead, which coincides with Jesus's return.

Back to Romans 11. What did Paul write concerning the *fullness* of the Gentiles and how that relates to Israel's *fullness*?

3. Read Romans 11:25 and write out your answers.

   a. What is the mystery?

   _____

   _____

   b. How long will the mystery last?

   _____

   _____

What is the fullness of the Gentiles? There are different interpretations.

- Some scholars believe it's a number—as in, we're waiting for all the Gentiles who will be saved to come to salvation. Revelation 7:9 presents the scene of people from every nation, tribe, people, and tongue before God's throne, yet today, there are still people who have never heard the gospel.

- Some believe the *fullness* speaks of unity and coming to the fullness of the knowledge of God (John 17; Eph. 4:13; Col. 1:28). That certainly hasn't happened yet.

> *Your kingdom come. Your will be done, on earth as it is in heaven. (Matt. 6:10)*

Either way, the fullness of the Gentiles is not yet complete and, therefore, the partial hardening of Israel is still in effect.

IT'S A PROCESS

What is certain is the fullness for both Gentiles and Israel is a process that is presently involved.

We can be sure of this because every day more and more people from every nation and tribe of the world are receiving the gospel in their own language and coming to salvation in Jesus. Entire ministries are devoted to the translation and distribution of the Bible. We're in an "already-and-not-yet" continuum.

The fullness of Israel is also in process. In 1948 there were about two dozen Jewish believers living in Israel. Today, some estimate the number to be up to 50,000. Additionally, thousands more Jewish believers live outside of Israel, and the number is growing. More Jews are coming to faith in Jesus today than in all the centuries combined since Jesus's day. But it's still a remnant of believers, not *all Israel yet*. Israel's fulfillment is in an "already-and-not-yet" state.

Oh, but there is hope for both!

In astronomy, Venus is called the morning star. It's the planet closest to Earth and appears brightest in our eastern sky right before dawn. Astronomers say if you see the morning star, take hope because it's the promise that the full day is coming.

4. What does Jesus call Himself in Revelation 22:16?

_____

If Jesus, our "morning star," came the first time and fulfilled His assignment as the Lamb of God, take hope and be sure the fullness is coming. He will return and fulfill every good purpose and promise as King! His righteousness will be established, and His family will come to its fullness—Jew and Gentile, sons and daughters of Abraham by faith, who are the sons and daughters of God. It's one family with distinctions.

JESUS'S RETURN

> *For I consider that the sufferings of this present time are not worthy to be compared with the glory that is to be revealed to us. For the anxious longing of the creation waits eagerly for the revealing of the sons of God. (Rom. 8:18–19)*

Even if some people don't know of the hope of the coming fullness when Jesus returns, the earth knows it!

On the day of Pentecost, Peter preached that Jesus would remain in heaven "until the period of restoration of all things about which God spoke by the mouth of His holy prophets from ancient time" (Acts 3:21).

The earth is waiting. Jesus is waiting. Are you waiting for Him?

Listen to the cry of the prophet Isaiah: "Oh, that You would rend the heavens and come down, that the mountains might quake at Your presence" (Isa. 64:1).

Jesus said that before His return, the gospel will be preached in the whole world, to all nations, and then the end will come (Matt. 24:14).

He said He will not return until the Jewish leaders in Jerusalem call for Him, saying, "BLESSED IS HE WHO COMES IN THE NAME OF THE LORD!" (Matt. 23:37–39).

> *And so all Israel will be saved; just as it is written, "THE DELIVERER WILL COME FROM ZION, HE WILL REMOVE UNGODLINESS FROM JACOB." (Rom. 11:26)*

The greatest spiritual awakening is about to happen; the greatest revival is on its way! World events are building up to it now, and we will continue to see everything take shape. The birth pangs will intensify before the Lord's return, and, yes, there will be perilous days, but Jesus said, "See that you are not frightened" (Matt. 24:6). Isaiah cried out, "Arise, shine; for your light has come, and the glory of the LORD has risen upon you. For behold, darkness will cover the earth and deep darkness the peoples; but the LORD will rise upon you" (Isa. 60:1–2).

Imagine the explosive effect within creation when the *fullness* is as it needs to be—whatever exactly that is. King Jesus will arise from His throne and the heavens will be split; the clouds will be rolled back like a scroll. *What kind of moment will that be?!*

5. We encourage you to read this progression of the Lord's return. Let the Word of God speak.

    a. Revelation 19:7, 11–16
    b. Matthew 24:29–31
    c. 1 Corinthians 15:51–57
    d. Zechariah 12:3, 8–10; 13:1
    e. Ezekiel 36:25–28
    f. Ezekiel 39:29
    g. Romans 11:26–36

The fullness of the Gentiles will be realized. The partial hardening of Israel's heart will be removed! Anyone alive at that time who is a part of Abraham's natural family will receive Jesus: *all Israel will be saved.* Regarding these natural branches of the olive tree that had been broken off because of unbelief, Paul wrote, "God is able to graft them in again" (Rom. 11:23).

REFLECTION

The future hope of Israel is intimately tied to the future hope of the believer. The coming revival and great awakening will crescendo until the sky splits apart and the King comes in the clouds.

The family, in its *fullness*, will be the pure and spotless bride of Jesus, whom He will present to Himself (Eph. 5:27).

6. Read Matthew 24:6; Matthew 25:13; 1 Corinthians 15:58. What is our posture to be while we wait for the *fullness* to come?

   _____

   _____

7. Write out your thoughts, perhaps a prayer to the Lord, regarding all you've read in the Word these two days.

   _____

_____

_____

_____

_____

_____

_____

Friends, we recognize and deeply respect the various interpretations and opinions regarding the last days, the Church's place in them, and Israel's salvation. In no way do we intend to be dogmatic in our presentation of this material but rather to evaluate key Scripture passages and concepts with humility and hope for the days ahead. We recognize that no one has every detail, the timing, or the progression of the last days nailed down perfectly. That said, it's also been a disservice to believers and to the lost world over the years to avoid talking about the Lord's return and His kingdom for fear of getting it wrong or offending anyone. *It's the good news! This is the hope of Israel and the great expectation of the Church.*

FURTHER STUDY

To learn more about our shared hope for the coming revival, scan this QR code to read Dr. Jürgen Bühler's article, "God's Promises for Israel's Restoration."

DAY 3
HOPE IN THE WAITING

Maybe you've heard this statement: *What you believe will determine how you live.* It's true.

Now may the God of hope fill you with all joy and peace in believing, so that you will abound in hope by the power of the Holy Spirit. (Rom. 15:13)

We've highlighted Abraham throughout this course because he is the father of Israel and the father of all who are of faith, Jews and Gentiles. He's called the "friend of God" in the context of honoring Abraham's belief in all God promised, which resulted in righteousness (James 2:23). What did Abraham believe that so ordered how he lived?

Today, we'll focus primarily on Abraham's example of holding on to hope even when the period of waiting for the fulfillment is long-delayed.

1. What is the definition of faith according to Hebrews 11:1?

2. What would strong faith look like? Conversely, how would a lack of faith affect how someone might live?

Before we get into Hebrews 6, let's think again about the believer's hope. What does it entail? Yes, the answer is *Jesus*. That's usually the great answer—isn't it? But let's expand it to include what Jesus has done and what He will do, according to the broad brush of prophecy.

THE BELIEVER'S HOPE

- Jesus died for our sins, was raised again to life, and defeated sin and death (Acts 2:23–24).
- He removed our curse of sin and clothes every believer with His righteousness and eternal life (Rom. 6:22–23; Col. 3:10).
- He has given us His Holy Spirit, who is with us forever (John 14:16–17; Acts 2:33).
- He's at the right hand of the Father in heaven, ever living to make intercession on our behalf (Heb. 7:25).
- He will return to earth for His own and to judge the unbelieving world (2 Thess. 1:6–10).
- He will gather the saints to Himself, and we will always be with Him (1 Thess. 4:16–17).
- There will be a resurrection of both the saved and the unsaved (1 Cor. 15:20–23; Rev. 20:12).
- He will establish His eternal kingdom (Dan. 7:27).
- He will destroy Satan and death (Rev. 20:10, 14).

There could certainly be more listed here, but the above is part of what the Bible describes as our hope.

> *There is a bringing in of a better hope, through which we draw near to God (Heb. 7:19).*

3. Read Hebrews 6:11–20 and answer the questions.

   a. verse 11: What was the writer's desire?

   _____

Note: The writer speaks of a "full assurance of hope," or a "sure hope," depending on your translation. The idea means to have complete confidence in, conviction of, or being fully convinced of something, in this case, of the hope of all things that accompany our salvation—the list under "The Believer's Hope" above. And there's more!

   b. verses 12, 15: Why is diligence in laying hold of the full assurance of hope important? How are the promises obtained?

   _____

   _____

   c. verses 13, 16–18: God speaking the promises to Abraham would have been enough, for He cannot lie. But to underscore that He would do what He promised, God took an oath. According to what did God swear?

   _____

   _____

We don't know exactly what Abraham knew regarding the full scope of God's plan. He knew enough, though. He saw Jesus's day (John 9:56). He believed in God's ability to raise the dead (Heb. 11:17–19). He looked for God's eternal city with foundations "whose architect and builder is God" (Heb. 11:10).

The promises and truths of God are a progressive revelation. No prophet or biblical writer received the full picture but carried that which God entrusted to them. We live in the remarkable day of having the complete Word of God and the indwelling Holy Spirit—things Abraham didn't have. It's breathtaking.

d. verse 19: What is our hope likened to, and how is it described?

Note: Your soul is the combination of your mind, will, and emotions.

REFLECTION

No matter what storms come our way, we are anchored in the immutable, unchanging, Word of God, by the power of the Holy Spirit. We can have a sure hope that He will do what He says.

4. What does it mean that our souls are anchored by the hope set before us (Heb. 6:18)? What might an "anchored" soul look like?

5. If we do not lay hold of the hope set before us and let go of the truths listed above in "The Believer's Hope" section, how will our souls (mind, will, emotions) be affected?

6. Have you laid hold of the hope set before you—all of it? How's your soul?

___

Hope does not disappoint, because the love of God has been poured out within our hearts through the Holy Spirit who was given to us. (Rom. 5:5)

7. Read the *In Essence* lesson summary provided at the beginning of Lesson 7. As you have considered the future hope of Israel, have further questions come to mind? Or perhaps you've experienced poignant moments where some dots were connected. If so, write them out.

___

FURTHER STUDY

To learn more about hope in the Bible, scan this QR code to read Esther Kuhn's article, "Hope in Hebrew: Tikvah—Hope That Does Not Disappoint."

LESSON 8
WHAT'S OUR ROLE? THE NOT-SO-FINE PRINT OF THE GREAT COMMISSION

IN ESSENCE

Jesus fully surrendered to His heavenly Father and did nothing on His own initiative but only what He saw the Father doing. He called His disciples to "Follow Me" (i.e., Matt. 9:9). When we're aligned with Jesus, we'll be aligned with the Father's heart, and our feet will follow into daily action. The things on God's heart will be on ours.

Israel, God's firstborn, is today far from home and with limited ability to find the way back without help. The Father has asked us, His children by faith, to go and bring His son home. We've been summoned by the Father to step further into the story of Israel's restoration. Will we do it? Will we share the hope of the gospel with Jewish family and friends? Will we pray for the veil to be lifted from their eyes?

GETTING STARTED

Group leader, read the In Essence *summary as you begin your time together. This will help set up the direction for this lesson.*

As you open the group time, give everyone an opportunity to answer this question:

> ▶ How would you get the word out quickly if you had to? (What "the word" is and what "quickly" means is open to personal interpretation.)

God chose you and me to partner with Him to get the greatest word, the gospel, to every nation—including back to the Jewish people, the original carriers.

 LESSON 8 VIDEO

Group leader, stream the video lesson using the QR code on page 3.

As you watch the video teaching, use the following prompts and space provided to record anything that stands out to you.

> *Then He said to me, "Son of man, these bones are the whole house of Israel; behold, they say, 'Our bones are dried up and our hope has perished. We are completely cut off.'" (Ezek. 37:11)*

1. "What would Jesus do?"

2. God is asking each of us to step further into the story of Israel's restoration.

3. Ezekiel's first assignment, a mandate for us as well, was to prophesy to the bones—to speak to Israel, saying, "Hear the word of the LORD" (37:4).

4. Prophesy to the breath. Call for the Holy Spirit to breathe spiritual life into the bones. *Pray!*

5. Would you allow God to break your heart for Israel?

6. God, help us to be so like Jesus that the sound of our cry melds with His.

> *For the brokenness of the daughter of my people I am broken. (Jer. 8:21)*

GROUP DISCUSSION QUESTIONS

Group leader, read the following questions and prompts out loud and lead the discussion.

As we begin the final discussion of *Love What God Loves*, let's summarize what we've covered so far, which will then lead us into the discussion questions below.

- God is establishing a people for Himself. It's an international family of faith made possible by the blood of Jesus and His indestructible life.
- God chose Abraham and his natural family, Israel, as vessels through whom the revelation of God, His plan of salvation, and the Messiah would be offered to the world.
- Gentile believers in Jesus are grafted into Abraham's family by faith and become co-heirs with Israel of the promises and partakers in the Great Commission of making disciples of Jesus in every nation.
- Over the millennia, Satan has made countless efforts to derail God's purposes by silencing and eliminating Israel (the messengers), disqualifying Jesus, and dividing Abraham's family of faith. But God will uphold all His purposes. We have a blessed hope.

Discuss these questions.

1. The Church, made up of Jewish and Gentile believers, is God's Plan A in reaching the world with the gospel. Who is God's Plan A in reaching the Jewish people with that message? Read Romans 11:11–14.

Several years ago, a Messianic Jewish ministry conducted a survey and asked a cross section of Jewish believers how they came to faith in Jesus. Ninety percent reported they did so through the friendship and influence of a Gentile friend.

Read Ezekiel 37:1–8 and answer the questions below.

2. How confident are you in sharing the gospel with Jewish friends or family members? Is there a degree of fear and uncertainty involved? If so, discuss it within your group.

It's possible some group members may not yet have had the chance to befriend a Jewish person. We encourage you to ask the Lord to bring His people into your life.

3. What are the most effective ways to share your faith with others—Jewish or not? Are there nuances when sharing your faith with a Jewish person?

Read Ezekiel 37:9–14 and answer the questions below.

4. Has your prayer life been affected as you've participated in *Love What God Loves*? If so, in what way(s)?
5. Read Isaiah 62:11–12. What are we called to proclaim?
6. Over the years and in various circles, there has been criticism or concern that too much emphasis on Israel gives the impression of divine favoritism. What are your thoughts on that? Is it an issue of favoritism or God's faithfulness?
7. What is your primary take-away from *Love What God Loves*?

CONCLUSION

When we see Israel through the Father's eyes, we'll find people waiting, whether they know it or not, for the Church to present a true and loving witness of Jesus, their Messiah. All believers are summoned into this calling to some degree. Israel is God's firstborn, and He is passionate for their restoration—not because of favoritism but according to His name and faithfulness to His promises.

Will you prophesy to the bones (speak to the Jewish people) and give them the gospel?

Will you prophesy to the breath (pray) on their behalf?

CLOSE IN PRAYER

As you close your group's time together, see if anyone needs prayer, and take a few minutes to cover those requests.

Since the Church is Plan A for seeing the Jewish people come to know the Lord, pray that the Lord will bring more Jewish people into your paths.

Pray for opportunities to share with others what you've learned from *Love What God Loves: Seeing Israel through the Father's Eyes*.

PERSONAL STUDY BETWEEN SESSIONS

This section is designed for your personal study to help you dig deeper into some of the themes from the teaching and discussion.

DAY 1

TO THE JEW FIRST

Do you remember this famous phrase from our parents: "Because I said so!" Many of us committed to never using it. It's doubtful we were successful. Sometimes it's just the best answer.

We might be tempted to employ "because God said so" to answer the question of why the gospel is to the Jews first. Hear Paul's words in Romans 1:16:

> For I am not ashamed of the gospel, for it is the power of God for salvation to everyone who believes, to the Jew first and also to the Greek.

Paul, under the inspiration of the Holy Spirit, prioritized the gospel going to the Jewish people. Why?

> *The word "first" in the Greek is proton (πρῶτον) and speaks of priority and not just a chronological order.*

God is a God of order. We see it in the natural world with time and seasons, animal migration—endless examples. God set an order within the family and in our finances. We see detailed purpose and order in the building of Moses's Tabernacle, and God established order to the gospel: to the Jew first.

In the Old Testament Law, the "firsts" were important to the Lord.

1. What do you learn about every firstborn and first fruits of the harvest in Exodus 13:1–2 and Exodus 22:29–30?

   Read Leviticus 27:30. What do you learn about the tithe (first 10 percent)?

2. What is Israel called in Exodus 4:22?

The firstborn opened the womb of the mother with the expectation and hope of more children. In a similar way, Israel opened God's "womb," if you will, with the expectation of more spiritual sons and daughters.

Jesus is called the "first fruits" of those who have been raised from the dead, but the great expectation is the resurrection of the dead at His return (1 Cor. 15:20, 23). It's the same pattern of expectation: more will follow.

The firstborn was "holy" to the Lord, which doesn't mean "perfect" but rather "set apart." Israel was called a holy nation—not perfect but set apart for purpose.

3. Though it may be a review, read these verses and note God's purpose for Israel. What did He call His people?

   a. Isaiah 43:1, 10; Acts 1:8

b. Isaiah 41:8–9

_____

_____

c. Isaiah 42:6; Matthew 5:14

_____

_____

God perfectly fashioned and prepared Israel by revealing Himself and His truth. No other nation had the message of *one God*—monotheism. Instead, the world worshiped many false gods. No other nation received the revelation of God's holiness and the message of life being in the blood and a substitutionary sacrifice for sin—only Israel, when God gave the Torah. God gave Israel the covenants, the Scriptures, the prophecies, and the promise of a Messiah, the Anointed One, who would carry our sin away, heal our diseases, and reign as King. No other nation was looking for a king from Bethlehem, from David's lineage—only Israel. The Holy Spirit gave Daniel the timeframe for the Messiah's appearance. No one else had this.

> *The gifts and the calling of God are irrevocable. (Rom. 11:29)*

God had also perfectly prepared Israel to receive Jesus, which is why Jesus was often angry at the religious leaders for not discerning the signs of the times, the days in which they lived. They should have known, but so many didn't.

Today, Israel is mostly separated from the Father except for the wonderful believing remnant. The Father wants His son home. He wants the light relit. The servant needs to again be about the Father's business of carrying the gospel to the ends of the earth.

The late Elie Wiesel, a Holocaust survivor and author, once compared modern Jewry to a messenger who had been hit on the head and knocked out. When he woke up, he couldn't remember the message, who had sent him, to whom he had been sent, or the very fact that he was a messenger.

The Father wants His messenger to carry His message. The Jewish people *have* a message, and they *are* a message. They are a message of God's faithfulness—not favoritism, faithfulness.

4. Read Ezekiel 36:19–23. On what basis can we be sure God will uphold His promises?

   Read also verses 32–36. Who also benefits when Israel is restored to the Father?

REFLECTION

"To the Jew first" was Jesus's ministry pattern (Matt. 15:24). It was the order He gave to His disciples (Matt. 10:5–6). It was the pattern the apostle Paul followed, although he was an apostle primarily to the Gentiles. When he entered a new city, he went to the synagogue first before turning to the Gentiles (Acts 13:5, 46; 14:1).

5. Below is a quote from a participant in a focus group for this course. Does it resonate?

   I'm troubled at why I am treating these people as "other" and considering them "could-have-been Christians" and "those who rejected Jesus" instead of evangelizing them. Tonight, I've been forced to confront what is in my subconscious.

6. When you read or hear that the priority of the gospel is "to the Jew first," what thoughts come to your mind?

Let's trust God's divine order and His perfect heart of love. At the end of the day, if the above isn't convincing, we can always agree the gospel is to the Jew first "because God said so."

▷ FURTHER STUDY

To learn more about God's priority pattern of "to the Jew first," scan this QR code to read the article by FIRM staff, "To the Jew First: The Meaning of Romans 1:16."

DAY 2
ENTERING THE TRAVAIL

It's true in the natural and the spiritual: *birthing comes with a travail*.

1. Paul counted all things as loss in view of the surpassing value of knowing Jesus. Read Philippians 3:10 and note what Paul desired to know about the Lord.

2. Read Colossians 1:24. What was Paul's response to suffering? What was he willing to do?

> Some have said the Church needs a "baptism of tears"—a baptism of deep repentance—to purge us of pretense, unify our hearts, and perceive what the Spirit is saying.
>
> The same can be said for the Church toward Israel. To see the spiritual awakening of the Jewish people, tears are needed—only a baptism of tears for Israel can wipe away the stain of blood, speaking of the Jewish blood spilled in the name of the Church since the early centuries.

LESSON 8: WHAT'S OUR ROLE?

In Isaiah 25:6 we read of a magnificent banquet prepared on Mount Zion that the Lord will prepare for His bride—it's the marriage supper of the Lamb. It's a beautiful and sure hope we have, but in verses 7–8, we learn what must be swallowed up—that which has covered all peoples, a veil that has stretched over all nations. In verse 8, the Lord will "swallow up death for all time." Even the wedding feast will come only after the travail over death is finally over.

Birthing, bringing something to life, involves pain and resilience. We must have a vision for what God wants to accomplish and a steel dedication to see it through. Jesus is our example, who for the joy set before Him, "endured the cross, despising the shame" (Heb. 12:2).

Will you allow God to break your heart for what breaks His? Are you willing to enter the travail for the lost in every nation? Would you step into the travail for Israel's salvation? Would you have God allow you to feel the pain the Jewish people have experienced? The Bible says God weeps with those who weep.

If this is something you're ready to do, we encourage you to use your own words, even now, and ask the Lord to reveal His heart to you. Tell Him you're willing to join His travail over His lost sons and daughters.

If we're to see Israel through the Father's eyes, what will we see?

3. Read Jeremiah 8:21–22; 9:1, 10–20. Summarize Israel's condition and God's heart.

_____

_____

_____

_____

> *Thus says the* LORD *of hosts, "Consider and call for the mourning women, that they may come; and send for the wailing women, that they may come! Let them make haste, take up a wailing for us, that our eyes may shed tears and our eyelids flow with water." (Jer. 9:17–18)*

There is a beautiful tribe of people in Kenya called the Maasai. They are expert herdsmen, and it's critical for the family financially and socially to maintain their cattle. The Maasai women are known for their ability to communicate house to house through distinctive cries and wails. Different cries carry different messages. One unique wail becomes a desperate cry for help when the man discovers one of his cows has been stolen. The woman of the house will let out the distinct cry, a call to the neighbor, "The cow has been stolen! Come!" The women carry the wailing message from house to house, and the villagers will come running and coordinate their efforts to recover the lost cow.

> *Now, you women, hear the word of the LORD; open your ears to the words of his mouth, teach your daughters how to wail. (Jer. 9:20 NIV)*

Oh, how much more is the value of a son or daughter, lost in sin and darkness.

Jesus wept over Jerusalem; the people were like sheep without a shepherd. Paul had "great sorrow and unceasing grief" (Rom. 9:2) in his heart for his kinsmen, natural Israel, who were separated from the Messiah. Jeremiah wept over Israel's condition. God wept. Will you?

REFLECTION

4. Read Psalm 126:1–6. What is the promise in verses 5–6?

   _____

   _____

5. Close your time today in prayer asking the Holy Spirit to reveal His heart to you regarding His lost son.

   > *Blessed are you who weep now, for you shall laugh. (Luke 6:21)*

   Thus says the LORD, the Holy One of Israel, and his Maker: Ask Me about the things to come concerning My sons, and you shall commit to Me the work of My hands. (Isa. 45:11)

   _____

LESSON 8: WHAT'S OUR ROLE?

_____

_____

_____

_____

If you have time and want to see more of God's heart regarding the lost and His joy over those being found, read Luke 15, where Jesus presents the parables of the lost sheep, the lost coin, and the lost son.

▶ FURTHER STUDY

To learn more about how to pray for Israel and the Jewish people, scan this QR code to read the article by FIRM Staff, "How Do I Pray for Israel? 3 Helpful Tips."

DAY 3
SHAMMAH THE SON OF AGEE A HARARITE

In our final *Personal Study* section for *Love What God Loves*, let's widen the view to again see the big picture of what God is doing on the earth and how our individual lives are deeply connected to His story. *You matter in God's story, and you affect God's story!*

In Lesson 1, Michael shared that the prophecy in Genesis 3:15 reveals God's plan on our behalf. In the garden of Eden, after the fall of man, God spoke these words to the serpent (Satan):

> *I will put enmity between you and the woman, and between your seed and her seed; He shall bruise (crush) you on the head, and you shall bruise him on the heel.*

The Lord Himself—the seed of the woman, the Son of God—will crush Satan's head. It's a progressive revelation throughout the entire Bible as to how God will accomplish it, through whom, the connecting promises and provisions, the pitfalls, and the ultimate restoration of all things ever intended to be restored! *What a story!*

What drives God to move on our behalf like this? *Love*. The Father is a God of love, and He desires a family for Himself in a renewed creation with no more sin or effect of sin. And He will have it.

We've used the visual of a family throughout this course. God also uses an agrarian term to express what He's doing. He is working toward and readying all things for the time of the great, ultimate harvest.

1. Read these verses about the harvest and write out what you learn.

    a. Matthew 13:24–30, 36–43

    _____

    _____

    b. Matthew 9:37–38

    _____

    _____

    c. John 4:35–36

    _____

    _____

The harvest of souls, the family of God, is in an "already-and-not-yet" process. Now is a time of harvest—today if you hear His voice, respond! Now is the time of salvation, but there's coming a day when Jesus will return for the ultimate harvest at the end of the age. He's passionate about it, eager to return, and desires that all would come to the Father through faith. *For God so loved the world.*

> *Pray. Go. Bring the sons and daughters back to the Father.*

Along the way, the good seed of the Word of God has come to you. If you've given your life to Jesus and received His gift of forgiveness and eternal life, He's called you into His story.

He wants each of us to arise and take our appropriate place, fulfill our role on His behalf, clear our throat, and give voice to the message of God's love and salvation through His Son, Jesus.

2. Read Romans 12:1–2, then write out Paul's exhortation to believers.

    _____

3. Read 2 Corinthians 5:20. What are we called and what is our calling?

King David was known as a great warrior with a select group of men in his company who were like the special forces. Men of renown. Men of passion and dedication. Men who understood sacrifice. They were known as "David's mighty men."

4. Read 2 Samuel 23:11–12 about Shammah and note below what he did.

Shammah's story is true—it happened in the natural—yet it teaches us a spiritual lesson. There was a field full of lentils, a harvest that needed protecting. The enemy was violent, and the people were afraid and ran, but not Shammah. He remained in the middle of the field, stood his ground against the enemy, and defended that harvest. His love for the king compelled him.

Shammah's name means "desert."
His father's name, Agee, means "I shall increase."
He was called a Hararite, meaning "mountain dweller."

Shammah's name speaks of dryness, barrenness, or being without water. It's the same condition of our lives before we met the Lord. But we have a heavenly Father whose all-sufficient supply is ready to pour into our lives—He will bring His increase into us. He will set His Spirit within us. He will forgive us. He will be our healing. He will wash and refresh us with the water of His Word. Because of the Lord, we are meant to be mountain dwellers, living on the heights, protected, with tremendous vision. *Arise, barren one, and be filled to overflowing.* For love of King Jesus, take your place in the middle of the field, which is the world, and defend His harvest.

Stay awake. Be alert. Pray. Have a tool in one hand and a sword in the other. Even if everyone around you runs in fear, will you stand? Jesus's return is near! There is a harvest today, but the ultimate harvest is coming. Will you give your life for His story?

REFLECTION

5. What is your response to Shammah's example? Write out your thoughts below.

6. Read the *In Essence* lesson summary provided at the beginning of Lesson 8. As you have considered your role in Israel's restoration, have further questions come to mind? Or perhaps you've experienced poignant moments where some dots were connected. If so, write them out.

We thank you from Jerusalem for sharing this time in the Word with us and participating in *Love What God Loves: Seeing Israel through the Father's Eyes*. Thank you for considering God's full story for creation, our individual roles as sons and daughters by faith, and most importantly, Israel's role in that story.

We pray you've seen Israel through the Father's eyes. We especially pray you've seen the Father and the Son in clearer ways.

If this course has added value to your walk with the Lord, we ask that you share it with others. Let's prepare the way for the Lord's return.

> *The LORD bless you, and keep you; the LORD make His face shine upon you, and be gracious to you; the LORD lift up His countenance upon you, and give you peace. (Num. 6:24–26)*

WE EXIST TO SEE A DAY WHEN EVERY PERSON IN ISRAEL IS TRANSFORMED BY THE LOVE OF JESUS.

Over the past decade, we've had the privilege of distributing millions of dollars to support effective ministry initiatives and projects. Together, we have a vision for a stronger and healthier body of Messiah in Israel.

We believe Israel can make an impact on everyone's life, and everyone has a role to play in Israel's story.

ABOUT FIRM

Fellowship of Israel Related Ministries (FIRM) is a global family of believers empowering local ministries to see every person in Israel transformed by the love of Jesus.

Based in Jerusalem, **we serve a network of seventy-five ministries and organizations in Israel** that share a passion for reaching Israelis with the love of Jesus.

We connect believers around the world to Israel while strengthening local ministries in the land.

Find out more about our work
FIRMISRAEL.ORG

THE TRIBE

Help transform lives in Israel every month.

WHAT IS THE TRIBE?

The Tribe is a global community of passionate monthly donors committed to transforming lives in Israel with the love of Jesus. Together, we partner with local believers to share the gospel and see lives changed.

HERE'S WHY THOUSANDS OF CHRISTIANS HAVE JOINED THE TRIBE:

- **100% Impact:** Every dollar you give directly supports gospel-centered ministry in Israel, with operating costs privately funded.

- **Real Stories:** Receive monthly updates and witness the life-changing impact of your generosity.

- **Be Part of God's Plan:** Join believers from every nation in God's mission to bring transformation to Israel through the love of Jesus.

Over 2,000 people have joined THE TRIBE so far.

Will you join them?
FIRMISRAEL.ORG/THETRIBE

NOTES

1. "Jewish Affinity Bloc," *Joshua Project*, accessed December 11, 2024, *https://joshuaproject.net/affinity_blocs/15*.

2. "When Things Seem out of Control – A. W. Tozer," *Deeper Christian Quotes*, accessed December 29, 2024, *https://deeperchristianquotes.com/when-things-seem-out-of-control-aw-tozer/*.

3. Ugo Bassi, quoted in Elisabeth Elliot, *Keep a Quiet Heart* (Grand Rapids: Revell, 2022), 64.

Made in United States
North Haven, CT
21 April 2025

68135062R00102